CW01500775

ABOUT EXTRAORDINARY BOOKS

Extraordinary Books is a not-for-profit company bringing a new approach to publishing. We were founded with a sense of outrage at the ever-growing monopoly exerted by the big publishers, and a desire to subvert the current state of the industry.

Here's what that looks like:

- We're seeking authors with something singular to contribute – a rare quality, a unique selling point, defying imitation. Whether an author has thousands of followers on social media or has never heard those two words joined before, we're committed. No platform? No problem.

- All our books receive equal, substantial attention and marketing budgets, and we share profits with our authors 50/50. As for us? We only need enough to keep publishing without compromise.

- We're guided by curatorial openness: our experienced team commissions books in-house, and our visionary editorial collective helps uncover singular writing.

Whether speculative fiction, art, memoir or anything in between, our books have this in common: a distinctive pairing of author and subject.

If that means publishing niche books, so be it. If it means going beyond the constraints of genre, we're up for that. If it means taking risks, bring it on.

We're for readers. *Not for profit.*

A COOL HEAD IN HELL

Extraordinary Books
Gable House, 18–24 Turnham Green Terrace
London W4 1QP
www.extraordinarybooks.co.uk

Published in Great Britain in 2025 by Extraordinary Books
Copyright © Jacqueline Passman, 2025

An earlier version of this work was published in 2020
by Tambar Arts, Ltd as *Harry's War*.
This edition has been revised and updated.

ISBN 978-1-917569-06-4
eISBN 978-1-917569-07-1

.EU GPSR authorised representative: Logos Europe
9 rue Nicolas Poussin, 17000 La Rochelle, France
contact@logoseurope.eu

Printed and bound in Great Britain by Clays Ltd, Elcograf S.p.a.

For Harry's children, grandchildren and great-grandchildren:
the family he wondered if he would ever have

A COOL HEAD
IN HELL

The Wartime Diaries of a British Doctor
from Dunkirk to the Burma Railway

HARRY SILMAN

Edited by Jacqueline Passman

CONTENTS

A NOTE ON LANGUAGE

This book contains numerous unedited passages from the personal diaries of Harry Silman, a British medical officer who was taken prisoner along with his comrades by Japanese forces during World War Two. In the interests of preserving the authenticity and historical integrity of his account, his use of language has been retained throughout as originally written, including terms that are now recognised as racist – such as those used when referring to his captors and their countrymen.

These pejorative terms, of course, reflect both the English-language vernacular of the time as well as prejudiced attitudes in general in North America, Europe and Oceania. Their use is not endorsed by the editor, Jacqueline Passman, or by the publisher; nor are they presented here to cause offence in any way. Readers are asked to approach the passages containing these terms with historical awareness and empathy.

Moreover, any inconsistencies and idiosyncrasies in general style, capitalisation, punctuation, italics, etc. are Harry Silman's own.

EDITOR'S NOTE

The core of this book comprises extracts from my father Harry's diaries and letters from his time with the British Expeditionary Force in France and his incarceration in the Far East. I have also transcribed Harry's observations in a documentary, *Back to the Front: Doctors at War*, produced by Yorkshire Television, based on an interview with him in 2003 when he was ninety-two years old.

There are several other sources for the material (see the section titled Sources and Notes for details). They include research by Louise and Paul Reynolds (the daughter and son-in-law of Padre Eric Cordingly, Harry's friend and fellow POW) and the objective viewpoint of Lt Jim Bradley RE, another friend from those days of captivity.

Harry Silman, graduation photo, c. 1933

Introduction

My father, Harry Silman, was born on 21 December 1910 in Leeds, the third of four children of Fanny and Reuben Silman. Harry was educated at Leeds Grammar School and Leeds University, where he studied medicine. After graduation he worked both as a general practitioner and at Leeds General Infirmary.

One of his first appointments was to a rural practice in Hawes, North Riding (now North Yorkshire). Here he conducted his rounds in a horse and cart and was frequently paid in kind with foodstuffs from his patients in the farming community. This was in the 1930s, before the creation of the National Health Service in 1948, which introduced free medical care for all. As was common for doctors at this time, he also did his own dispensing. His two most effective prescriptions were the same placebo: one blue and the other pink. Patients vowed that one worked much better than the other; it was a useful experience for Harry to see how the mind could affect the healing of the body. He would remember this when caring for fellow POWs in the Far East.

A highlight of his pre-war medical years was his four months' service as a ship's doctor on MS *Glenbeg*, a cargo ship with a return itinerary to the Far East. Merchant ships used to carry a few first-class passengers, who would be treated very much as cruise passengers are today. In addition to his medical duties, Harry was also expected to act as co-ordinator for onboard activities and entertainment for the benefit of these travellers.

The passengers disembarked at various ports, replaced by others. In this first of a series of letters to his family is Harry's typically tongue-in-cheek description of the initial intake:

2 MAY 1936

There are nine passengers viz: one married male – jovial and hearty – going out to plant rubber, by gad! and to shoot tigers, by Jove! Five married females going out to join their husbands in the far-flung corners of the empire and three single girls, ages varying from 19 to 23. The latter are bright young things and have to be kept well in hand. There are 2 dogs as cargo, and they are petted and exercised by each passenger individually. I'm sure they (the dogs) will soon expire from exhaustion.

By all accounts, Harry had great fun keeping the 'bright young things' well in hand.

His medical duties were varied:

20 MAY 1936

I attended a Chinese man with a lacerated hand.

He probably had been fighting with a knife against one of his fellow crew members. One of the lady passengers passed out from the heat and bumped her head a bit. She soon came round however under my expert ministrations. The Captain got a piece of metal in his eye and I spent about 30 minutes getting it out, and he is OK now.

He described a small surgical operation which, for various reasons, was clearly a low point in his medical services:

5 JUNE 1936

I got all the lumber and junk cleared out of the 'hospital' and I rigged up an operating table. This consisted of boards resting on soap boxes and covered with brown paper. I had to clean up and boil instruments in odd greasy pans, boil my gloves, get the anaesthetic ready and attend to hundreds of small details. I taught the second mate how to give an anaesthetic, and he acted as hon. anaesthetist very efficiently. The operation, under the circumstances, we carried out quite well, in spite of an enormous gallery of inquisitive Chinese sailors. The patient, in spite of my telling him to have no food before the operation, took no notice and ate a hearty lunch. Consequently halfway through the operation he proceeded to vomit copiously. This, combined with the smell of the pus, the hospital, the patient, the sailors, and not forgetting the fact that the temperature was a hundred and plenty in the shade made the afternoon a memorable one. All my attempts at asepsis were quite nullified by well-meaning helpers who fingered all my sterile instruments. However, I am pleased to relate, the patient is still living and is doing well. What a difference though, between operating in the Infirmary and operating here.

After travelling through the Suez Canal, he saw a big Italian passenger ship anchored close by:

14 MAY 1936

There were scenes of tremendous enthusiasm, cheering, clapping and waving of flags. I was told Mussolini's wife was on board, and all the Italian inhabitants of Suez had turned out to greet her. What a row there was. I filmed some of the scene.

By strange coincidence, Harry met up again with the captain of the *Glenbeg* six years later. Captain Newing was the pilot of the French ship *Félix Roussel*, which took Harry and his division into Singapore on 5 February 1942 and then left immediately, evacuating 1,100 Singaporean civilians.

When we were children, our father never spoke about what had happened during the war, and our mother told us not to ask any questions. I recently learned that the troops were specifically ordered not to talk about their experiences; the war in Europe was over, and people at home did not want to hear any more tales of suffering. By the end of the war the death rate for Western prisoners held by the Japanese was seven times higher compared to the numbers held in German POW camps – yet the events of World War Two in the Far East are nowhere near as well-known as those in Europe.

Louise Cordingly in *Echoes of Captivity* found that many former POWs under the Japanese had immense difficulties settling back into civilian life. They were psychologically damaged, suffering nightmares and flashbacks, which disturbed their families and caused long-term problems. However, this was not our family's experience. Harry was a cheerful, optimistic man, and it truly did not seem as if his time in captivity had affected him. All we knew was that he had eaten a lot of rice, suffered from recurring bouts of malaria and had had a girlfriend called One Lung Too Few (a joke typical of his wacky sense of humour).

In the 1980s our parents took a holiday in the Far East, which included a couple of days in Singapore. They had arranged in advance to have a tour of Changi Prison (now a civilian facility). Doing so had a cathartic effect on my father: after their return, he brought down an old leather case to show me memorabilia from his war years. I was fascinated to see not just diaries but also drawings and paintings, photographs, newspaper cuttings, medals, letters, telegrams, Japanese currency and a canvas roll containing his medical kit. It was a real treasure trove.

There is one small diary of his time in France and Belgium, containing mainly memos and jottings. The four diaries of his time in the Far East contain detailed descriptions of the capitulation and of life as a prisoner of war of Japan. The first three were small, three-month diaries – pharmaceutical company giveaways. To begin with, Harry wrote a daily entry on each page, but when he realised he would run out of paper, his writing became smaller and smaller. He then began writing more fully only on days on which he felt something of note had happened.

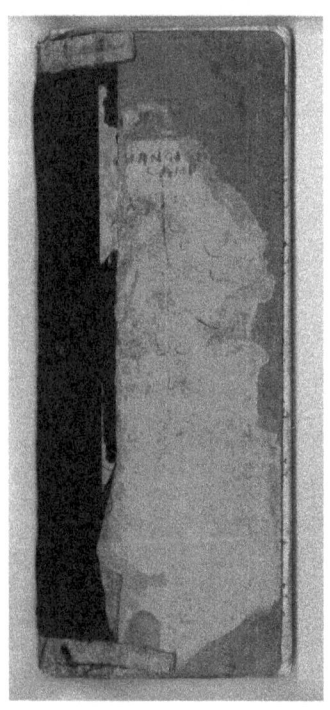

The cover of the fourth diary,
a partly used bill-of-lading

His supply of diaries ran out on Christmas Day 1942, but Harry was fortunate to find a partly used bill-of-lading book in which he wrote in both pen and pencil. The paper was very thin, so to start with he only wrote on one side of the page. When he reached the end, he turned it over to write on the other side. This did not make the diaries easy to read, particularly as his handwriting was a fairly typical doctor's scrawl. In addition, there were holes in several places where small sections had been deliberately cut out to destroy evidence of an illegal radio, which was a death penalty offence.

To keep a diary at all was strictly forbidden. Harry concealed his in various places, including under or sewn into his mattress. At one point, when he was at a camp on the Burma Railway, he was given a sudden order to move and did not have time to retrieve his diary. He was able to get a message to a friend, who brought it up to him some four weeks later.

Harry decided that parts of his diaries were worth transcribing. Some of the text in this book is based on his reading verbatim when we were together, and he would amplify the written entries. He dictated the rest of the section about the long trek up country and his time as medical officer (MO) on the railway (10 April 1943 to 22 December 1943), plus the incarceration at Selarang, onto a cassette, which I then transcribed and discussed with him to make sure it was accurate. The transcription was sent to the Imperial War Museum (IWM) and picked up by various organisations who found it of great significance.

The senior curator at the IWM replied that the diary entries

> are a happy mixture of personal and professional comment on your experience as a medical officer with the ill-starred F Force. You give a graphic picture of the appalling privations which you suffered during your journey to Bampong and forced marches to the top camps on the Burma–Siam railway, and a harrowing record of your efforts to combat the cholera epidemic and other diseases to which, because of the dreadful conditions, all the members of F Force were so vulnerable.

Harry thought that these were the only sections of his diaries which would be of interest to the general public, and so I transcribed about a fifth of the material with his help. After his death I felt it was important to complete the rest. It was a shock for my sister, brother and me to find out what our father had actually been through, as he had made light of his wartime experiences, joking about the hardships and privations as if they were mere inconveniences.

His articulate narrative of his time in captivity in the Far East presents acute observations, sometimes horrific, sometimes with flashes of his droll sense of humour. The diaries are now held in the IWM. His main diary was in a fragile state and has since been restored by the museum. The current senior curator there thanked the family for donating the diaries and commented on 'their detailed and eloquent account of the conditions endured by POWs in Japanese captivity. The diaries are amongst the best that I have so far read in this subject area.'

Jim Bradley sent my father a copy of his memoir, *Towards the Setting Sun*, recounting his attempted escape from the Burma Railway (see Chapter 13). He enclosed a letter in which he wrote that he always felt that my father was one of the great men in captivity.

In our family my father was one of the unsung heroes. He was an amazing man who went out of his way to care for people, something that continued throughout his life. I remember on more than one occasion he stopped the car when there appeared to have been an accident by the roadside. I also have holiday memories of him helping someone who was choking on a bone and going to hospital with a family whose child had broken their leg.

Harry retained to the end both the compassion and sense of humour which we believe helped him to survive as a POW. It is my privilege to tell his story, as much as possible in his own words.

Any further communication on this
subject should be addressed to:—
The Under-Secretary of State,
The War Office,
London, S.W.1.
and the following number quoted.

100/8/2570 (A.M.D.1.)

2nd January, 1940.

THE WAR OFFICE,
LONDON,
S.W.1.

SIR,

With reference to War Office letter dated ....8th December, 1939,........
No. 24/P.M.P./1924 (A.M.D.1.) I am directed to request that you will report
forthwith for duty to the

49th Anti-Tank Regiment,
Newcastle-on-Tyne.

You will be granted an emergency commission as Lieutenant, Royal Army
Medical Corps, from the date you join.

A list of articles of uniform you will be required to obtain is attached hereto,
together with the following pamphlets:—

(i) Arrangements for obtaining officers' uniform.

(ii) Pay and Allowances of officers, Royal Army Medical Corps.

You should not delay joining for the purpose of obtaining uniform and you
should take with you sheets, pillow cases and towels.

I am,
Sir,
Your obedient servant,

J. Robinson

Major,
for Director-General,
Army Medical Services.

Doctor.....H.Gilman,...............
.........86, Grange Avenue,...........
.................Leeds, 7.............

Copies to :—The General Officer Commanding-in-Chief, Command concerned.
The Officer Commanding the Unit concerned, who will forward the following to the
War Office when the officer has reported for duty :—
Arrival Report (Army Form B.151) showing date of reporting for duty and showing
also name and address of next of kin.—**Immediately**.
Army Form B.199A (original) as early as possible.

War Office commission as lieutenant, 2 January 1940

1

What a Night! ... Bombed, Machine-Gunned and Shelled

Harry enlisted as soon as war was declared in September 1939, and was posted to the 9th Battalion, Royal Northumberland Fusiliers (RNF). He was told to report immediately, so he set off in his old banger, which broke down in Darlington. He took a taxi to Newcastle but was upset to find that, far from expecting him, the reporting station did not yet exist, and he was put up in a hotel for three weeks. The battalion spent the winter training at Gosforth Park racecourse. Apparently, they were woefully underequipped. Although nominally a machine-gun battalion, they possessed only two machine guns, which were German weapons captured in 1918 that had been acquired by an officer of the regiment.

The early days of the war became known as the 'Phoney War', as there was little combat in western Europe. Those eight months gave the Allies time to train their troops in preparation for the battles that began when Germany invaded France in May 1940. The RNF, as part of the British Expeditionary Force (BEF), were sent to support the French.

They embarked on the SS *Fenella* at Southampton on St George's Day, 23 April 1940 – a significant day for the RNF, as their emblem features St George and the Dragon. St George was to be a potent symbol for the RNF during the war. In his wartime diaries – published in 2013 as *Down to Bedrock* – Padre Eric Cordingly named the chapels he consecrated in Singapore and Thailand after St George, and 'Fusilier George', author of the 9th Battalion RNF's period in France in 1940 – *A Story of the 9th Battalion, Royal Northumberland Fusiliers, April and May 1940* – chose it as his *nom de plume*. Even in captivity in Changi they celebrated St George's Day:

23 APRIL 1942

St George's Day dawned bright & clear (& very hot). We all went home & made roses in our hats – made out of red flags & white bandages. Everyone appeared to have a sparkle in their eyes. Special dinner with tablecloths – toast to the King & absent friends drunk in rum.

The RNF had the task of constructing an airfield. The week was divided into four days working on the airfields, two days training and a day of rest. The official history of the RNF states that 'as the role was a working and not a fighting one, the Division proceeded on a much-reduced scale of weapons, equipment and transport'. Although the two ancient machine guns had been supplemented by a further twenty-four plus an anti-tank rifle, they still had a 'skeleton scale of equipment'.

To begin with, there were few signs of war. They stayed in various small towns and villages and were welcomed by the French. The pseudonymous 'Fusilier George' wrote: 'Many and frequent were the bottles of wine that were cracked in celebration of our arrival to the furthering of the Entente Cordiale and to the speedy and utter downfall of the Hun.' There was a holiday atmosphere, and the army put on several variety concerts as entertainment. In that short period there were only a few medical problems requiring Harry's attention. Among others, he mentioned a fractured hand, bronchitis, pneumonia, scabies, a query appendicitis and two 'fake cases'.

After having lived under canvas since arriving in France, Harry was billeted in a *château* in Lillers, a small farming town around ten miles west of Béthune. There were constant air raid sirens, which were generally ignored. In an undated letter to his brother he wrote:

> Air raid warnings sound almost continuously but no one takes any notice now and most people appear rather bored. Our planes are certainly causing havoc among the Huns, but I think that we have a long way to go before we beat them.
>
> The chaps in my battalion are dying to use their guns on the Jerries & would welcome an opportunity of getting at them. The sad spectacle of thousands of

refugees heading south on every conceivable form of conveyance is seen from dawn till dusk every day now. Even dust carts and hearses are being used for this purpose.

The weather has kept very fine and sunny for the past two weeks and life is very pleasant. I am now sitting in the garden behind the Chateau in the hot sunshine with a Sapper book on one side, some chocolate on the other side and my writing pad on my knee.

Diary, 29 May 1940, Dunkirk: 'What a night!'

This almost idyllic rural existence ended abruptly when the German offensive began. 'Fusilier George' wrote:

> Friday 10th May 1940 will surely go down through the ages as one of the milestones of History. We were all awakened at about 0400 hours by the sound of heavy gunfire and the drone of internal combustion engines. The sky was dotted with small puffs of white smoke and there were to be seen a number of aircraft obviously of Hun extraction.

For the next few days the battalion went into defensive mode, presuming a parachute drop was imminent. The division was moved to the right flank of the BEF in preparation for an unexpected German advance. They were spread out into neighbouring towns, but all the roads were clogged with refugees.

The British troops then moved steadily northwards to reach Steenbecque, where they had the most intense combat of the war to date, defending the ridge which was becoming surrounded by German tanks:

24 MAY 1940

> Went into action against German tanks. We looked like being overwhelmed – troop carriers are reported to have landed. No sleep for 3 nights, must have affected the lads. Who can defend themselves against tanks with rifles? Where is the air force?

In a letter home on 4 June, Harry wrote: 'when we went into action against the Huns, we were actually surrounded by German tanks and got away by a miracle'. The following day the 9th RNF received this congratulatory message from Major-General Curtis:

> *WELL DONE!* If you had not held the STEENBECQUE ridge against tanks and infantry for 48 hours the Boches might now be in DUNKERQUE. The 9th have enhanced the tradition of the fighting 5th.

They were then ordered to withdraw, and retreated to Dunkirk under constant bombardment. On 28 May, Harry made a brief diary entry:

> Berthen. What a night! Travelling in the rain, bombed, machine-gunned and shelled. Hear that British army is evacuating this sector. Anticipate terrible slaughter on roads.

The following day they moved from Isenberg to De Panne:

> What a contrast – a bright sunny holiday crowd on the front and a few miles away there is a terrific battle. Took up positions near Ost Dunkirk, very heavily shelled. Living in beautiful houses on the seafront. Navy is protecting us with her AA guns.

Official photograph taken shortly after enlistment;
Harry inscribed it to his fiancée

It was total chaos on the beaches, so Harry took over a local café for his patients. There he delivered three babies to local women. He commandeered a truck to transport the sick and injured over the sand to the waiting boats. This was a difficult task as, apart from the constant bombing, he had to swerve frequently to avoid soldiers who, while they were waiting, part-buried themselves in the sand for protection with only their heads showing. In his letter home he said he could hear the shells and bombs bursting all around: 'It was a nightmare ride that I shall not forget in a hurry.'

Harry made several journeys from La Panne to Dunkirk before he ran out of fuel and walked the last stretch. He got away on the destroyer HMS *Malcolm*, accompanying the wounded he had rescued. A letter written by Montague Burton[1] to Harry's father praises Harry's 'bravery, self-possession and calmness in the firing-line'.

During the period between the retreat at Dunkirk in June 1940 and their departure for the eventual destination of Singapore in October 1941, the battalion was strengthened, properly equipped and trained in the UK. They were deployed first to defend the coastline in Devon and then Norfolk, waiting for a German invasion that did not materialise. They had further training in Scotland, Cheshire, Wiltshire and

---

1 Montague Burton was a highly respected Leeds businessman. He declined the offer to be Lord Mayor of Leeds but was knighted for services to industrial relations. He founded the tailoring business Burton Menswear, which, as the biggest UK tailoring business at the time, made a quarter of British military uniforms during World War Two.

North Wales. By the end of it, the official history of the RNF, *The History of the Royal Northumberland Fusiliers in the Second World War*, states that the 18th Division (of which the 9th Battalion was part) 'had become a highly-trained formation, and the RNF a first-class machine gun unit'.

Officers of the 9th Battalion during machine-gun training at Trawsfynnyd, North Wales, September 1941; Harry, lower R

2

Arrived at Singapore
After an Exciting Morning

Part of the battalion embarked at Greenock on 27 October 1941, and the rest of the 18th Division were picked up from Liverpool and Avonmouth two days later. Their planned destination was debatable, as the men had not been given this information. Harry and Padre Cordingly thought they were bound for Egypt, while Jim Bradley, an officer with the Royal Engineers (RE), said the most informed rumour was that they were heading for the Persian Gulf, with the object of linking up with the Russians in the Caucasus.

The British *Warwick Castle* was their first ship on the journey, taking them to Halifax in Nova Scotia. It was a roundabout route to avoid sailing near the European front. From Halifax they followed the coast of Canada and the eastern USA on the American *Orizaba*, protected by the United States Navy. At this time, the USA was not involved in the war, but there was an agreement that they would escort the British troops.

From there they sailed to Trinidad and arrived into Cape Town on 9 December.

Crucially, on 7 December, two days before the troops arrived in South Africa, the Japanese attacked Pearl Harbor, the US naval base in Hawaii. This took the military authorities by complete surprise, and immense damage was inflicted. It had the immediate effect of bringing the USA into the war. What is often forgotten is that on the same day, the Japanese also attacked the British base in Hong Kong and the RAF bases on the coast of the Malay Peninsula ('Malaya') to the north of Singapore, ensuring that the RAF would be unable either to retaliate or to protect their own troops. Britain declared war on Japan on 8 December. On 10 December the Japanese torpedoed Britain's naval forces, destroying the *Prince of Wales* and the *Repulse*, which were at the head of the fleet of ships sent to defend Singapore.

The sudden Japanese attack resulted in the 18th Division being diverted to defend the British military base on the island. They went via Mombasa to a camp at Deolali near Bombay (now Mumbai). They had set out prepared for desert fighting, with no provision for tropical conditions. In Deolali they had a fortnight's training, acclimatising and checking transport and equipment, but there were no inoculations against tropical diseases they might encounter. In reality, the troops were totally unequipped for a war in the Far East.

They set sail from Bombay on 23 January 1942 aboard the French ship *Félix Roussel*, arriving in Singapore on 5 February; it was already under heavy bombardment by the Japanese. The freighter that was carrying the battalion's transport did not manage to unload before it fled the bombing, so the RNF had to make do with requisitioned civilian vehicles. At the time the island of Singapore was thought to be impregnable, a fortress able to withstand any sea or air attack. To this end, there were huge gun fortifications which pointed south out to sea for the suspected invasion. The British newsreels and Churchill had imparted a general confidence that the British could protect Singapore, the 'City of the Lion', as it was one of the most strongly fortified bases in the world, and the many civilians living there had been assured they were safe. However, with both the air force and navy effectively out of action, it was easy for the Japanese to take advantage of the arrogant British belief that Singapore was invincible, and they attacked from the north via the supposedly impenetrable jungle – a way of entry dismissed by the British as being highly improbable.

Harry's Malaya Command ID

It is also possible that British HQ knew they were sending the 18th Division on a deployment that would prove to be a lost cause, but it was judged politically expedient that the Australian troops not be left to defend the island without support. In his diaries Harry reports on a talk by Major-General Beckwith-Smith on 23 April 1942:

> He praised the men for their part in that action on the island & hoped that we would soon show our true worth. Our coming to the island was a political and not a military fault.

It was a sacrificial gesture which led to a dreadful waste of life.

Singapore was virtually lost by the time the 18th Division arrived on 5 February 1942. However, apart from the noise of the shelling, there was none of the atmosphere of the war-torn Britain they had left behind with its blackouts and curfews. Bill Frankland said it did not seem like war at all, as all the lights were on and the city sparkled at night.[2]

There was a brief period of respite, and although the troops were getting used to hearing the Japanese barrage, they still had freedom of movement. In a much later diary entry Harry wrote about the loss of his camera and film footage taken at this time:

---

2 Bill Frankland was one of four veterans interviewed for *The Reunion: Far East Prisoners of War*, a Radio 4 programme recorded 26 April 2015 and presented by Sue MacGregor.

23 APRIL 1943

I was able to take some very interesting films during the battle and the immediate aftermath. I was very careful with the camera and the films. I sewed the camera and the films up in a canvas bag, and I decided to hide it somewhere until the end of the war. The padre took over a little mosque, next door to our billet. I climbed into the roof of the mosque into a circular dome. I pushed the camera and films into a very dark recess and I hoped to reclaim them after the war. Before I went up country, I went to check everything was there. Unfortunately, I found that someone had stolen it all. How someone knew it was there, or how it was spotted in the darkness, I do not know. Well that is that. I mourn the loss of the films more than the camera. The former are irreplaceable.

Harry had kept full diaries on the long voyage from the UK, but the day after capitulation, believing they might give military information to the Japanese:

I burnt all the souvenirs of the ships and also my diaries so conscientiously written up each day, covering the whole duration of the voyage.

This is the first entry of the diaries written in the Far East:

5 FEBRUARY 1942

Arrived at Singapore after an exciting morning with the Jap bombers. Two bombs hit the upper deck but did very little damage. Six killed & about 14 injured were our total casualties. I was in the aft RAP [Regimental Aid Post] and had a busy time for the duration of the attack. The *Empress of Asia* was bombed and caught fire, but all the crew and troops were taken ashore with very few casualties. The pilot of our ship was Capt Newing of the *Glenbeg* [the merchant ship Harry had served on in 1936 as ship's doctor]. Had short talk with him after the excitement had died down. Came into dock at night without tugs or shore help, & bumped the boat a few times but finally managed to get in. Aussies were waiting with trucks to take us to Hill 85 where we were to camp out. Had a bad cold and sleeping on damp grass without covering· didn't help any.

The next night Harry shared a tent with Padre Eric Cordingly. Their friendship had started in France and continued throughout their captivity in the Far East. In *Down to Bedrock* the Padre made the following comment about the man he called 'Doc':

We have been soldiering (an inapt term applied to us!) for three years and we have fought together in all senses of the word. He has a delightful sense of humour. Without knowing it, he often restores my sense of proportion.

Although they were from very different backgrounds, they had the same sense of purpose and a job of work to do.

The first nine days were spent collecting supplies and setting up medical arrangements, including a field ambulance:

7 FEBRUARY 1942

Set up MI Room [Medical Inspection room] in tent near main road and got unpacked as the packages were brought up by bit by bit from the docks. Only one bale of blankets was missing. The officers mess was a rather Heath Robinson affair consisting of bamboo poles, palm leaves and string. It made good cover and was well camouflaged. Several times during the day we had to jump quickly into slit trenches as the Jap bombers were overhead. Our seats at table consisted of ammunition boxes and the table made of planks resting on similar boxes. I never inquired if they were full but when bombers were overhead, I took no chances.

8 FEBRUARY 1942

The companies took up various positions round the camp and one company was detailed to join its brigade. My cold had improved considerably and I was able to wander about and get my medical arrangements working smoothly. Liaised with a nearby field ambulance for the evacuation of possible wounded. Newspapers brought up from Singapore kept us in touch with local and foreign news. We heard that the *Félix Roussel* had got away safely packed tight with civilian evacuees, mostly bound for Java or Australia. It is very hard for families to leave their houses, possessions and businesses, and go out into the unknown with just the money they can lay their hands on. Their furniture and chattels will be non-existent when they return.

9 FEBRUARY 1942

News received that the Japanese had effected a landing on the west coast and were advancing. This part of the coast had been defended by 'West Force' composed mainly of Australians who had fought on the mainland. They did not appear to offer much resistance to the landing forces. Consequently the Japs were able to land large forces without much hindrance and advanced eastward. The advance was preceded by a terrific barrage which we heard in the early hours of the morning and sounded like a continuous rumble.

One can imagine that this interim period must have been very difficult for the troops.

10 FEBRUARY 1942

Small arms fire was heard about 4 AM so we jumped into our clothes and stood to in the trenches until dawn. It seemed incredible that they could have penetrated so far so quickly but it may have been due to over-eager British forces. A lot of the firing on our part was unnecessary and due to 'nerves' – setting off the rest of the area into a flap. The Jap exploding bullets helped to create a state of confusion. In PM went with Major Leech & Hindmarsh to reccy new area, but spent most of the time lying flat and watching shells pass overhead both ways.

11 FEBRUARY 1942

Situation became incredibly serious as the news of the Jap advance came through. The RAP in one corner of the perimeter was dug down to a depth of 4 feet so that we could get stretchers under cover. Positions were manned constantly and patrols were sent out. The mess was below ground level and the batman helped by the Padre spent more of the day digging it deeper so we could sit and eat in spite of shelling overhead. Our table was a solid soil centre. Jap bombers were frequently overhead, but fortunately did not unload over our neighbourhood. British AA gunners put up a heavy barrage and I began to wonder how long the supply of shells would last. The water situation began to be a little difficult as it all had to be collected by hand.

By 12 February it was clear the situation was becoming grave. Yet even at this late stage it appears that events were not being taken as seriously as they should, and Harry records:

After the CO had spent a morning in conferences, he came back at lunchtime and told us to drop everything – take what we could carry and a packet of biscuits and prepare to move off. There was no cause for all this sudden flap except that Div were moving during the afternoon sometime. However we obeyed orders and I left all my cherished kit behind in my tent.

They slept in a tent that night. The next day was spent in the house which served as the mess. In spite of 'a morning of scares and shelling', Harry describes the mundane activities of washing and shaving, eating and drinking.

It seems scarcely believable that during the period before surrender the officers arranged a ball at Raffles Hotel. A photograph was taken of them in their dress uniform, and it was hanging in Raffles Hotel when my parents visited Singapore in the late 1980s.

Officers in Singapore, pre-capitulation,
February 1942: Harry, far L

3

Very Momentous Day

Much has been written about the fall of Singapore, with most historians and military analysts in agreement that Singapore was lost due to several catastrophic mistakes. On 6 December 1942 General Percival published an article in the local *Syonan Times* on 'Why We Were Defeated'. Harry commented:

> Percival says plainly that our troops were unseasoned, couldn't fight for long periods, lack of air support & absence of coastal defences on the north shore of Singapore. He also mentions the speed of the Jap advance which probably was too fast for our slowly moving army minds.

Churchill admitted it was the worst disaster and largest capitulation in British history. It was not the first time, nor unfortunately will it be the last, that thousands of lives were lost owing to disastrous military decisions.

One of the most horrific atrocities during this period was the brutal massacre of the medical staff and patients at the Alexandra Hospital in Singapore. On 14 February 1942 the hospital was under attack. A British medical officer wearing a Red Cross armband came out but was fired at. As he ran back in, he was followed by Japanese soldiers. They went from ward to ward, shooting, bayoneting or assaulting doctors, nurses and patients indiscriminately, including killing an anaesthetised patient who was waiting for an operation. Those who were not murdered in the hospital were either killed as they fled or rounded up and executed the following morning. In the post-war Japanese war crime trials, there was no evidence to prove the identity of the main perpetrators, and they were never brought to justice.

Although the British troops could clearly see the signs of what was to come, Harry's diary entry for 14 February is still fairly relaxed, in spite of the severity of the attack around him:

> Very busy day for me as the casualties came pouring in and the ambulance I had picked up was a godsend. The Padre stayed in the RAP and did good work cheering up the wounded. We buried one man behind our tent. Intense mortar fire made us crouch down most of the day and our tent was ripped by shrapnel many times. Meals in the mess were interrupted by bombing and a lovely evening meal was spoiled as we had to take cover for over an hour – being dark when we returned. Decided to get a good night's rest so slept in bed with sheets!

By the next day it was all over.

15 FEBRUARY 1942

Very momentous day. In morning had a good deal of attention from planes, guns and mortars and started to dig a deeper trench in the southern pit of the RAP. Numerous casualties including about 8 shell shock cases – the latter were packed off into the deep shelter. The ambulance worked splendidly getting the wounded away and the driver SB did very good work dodging shells and shell holes.

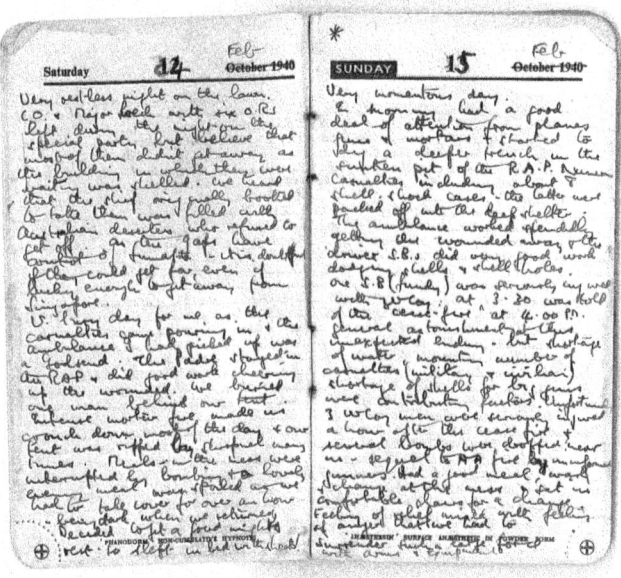

Diary, 15 February 1942, Singapore: 'Very momentous day'

General Percival took the decision to surrender. It is clear from Harry's diaries that this was not expected:

> At 3.30 was told of the 'ceasefire' at 4.00 PM. General astonishment at this unexpected ending – but shortage of water, mounting number of casualties (military and civilian), shortage of shells for big guns were contributing factors. Unfortunately 3 W Company men were seriously injured an hour after the ceasefire and several bombs were dropped near us – sequel to AA fire by uninformed gunners. Had a good meal, wash and change at the mess and sat on comfortable chairs for a change. Feeling of relief mixed with feeling of anger that we had to surrender such a large force with arms and equipment.

Padre Cordingly shared this feeling:

> It had been a nine-day wonder and while it lasted tense and exciting, but in reality rather more tragic and shattering. There was greatness in sacrifice and service, but war waged with modern weapons can have no glamour. We were stunned to hear we were to lay down our arms. I had wondered from time to time as the battle became fiercer; it seemed that this action would end in massacre or surrender ... I suppose the relief was terrific, there was that feeling that this ought not to be, we should not have been forced to lay down our arms, but the decision was

not ours, and we presume it had been taken after a review of the general position.

The day following the surrender, Harry went behind the Japanese lines with the Padre and a burial party to collect the casualties from the heavy bombing:

16 FEBRUARY 1942

Very difficult job as the bodies were swollen black and sizzling in the heat. The men in the Bren carriers were mangled and burnt, making identification impossible. We found one sergeant in a dug-out badly wounded, and by using a door managed to get him on to an ambulance. Saw a group of bodies covered over. We used slit trenches as far as possible as there was a lot of work to do. Took wounded sergeant to Sophia Road Hospital which was crowded out with cases. One Brigade including X Company were rounded up by the Japs and were herded in a field.

Approximately 100,000 British, Australian and Indian troops were marched seventeen miles to Changi, a former British military base in the north-east of Singapore island, to begin their three and a half years' captivity as prisoners of war.

'View from My Bed', Changi. Sketch by Harry Silman, July 1942

'My Billet', Changi. Sketch by Harry Silman, July 1942

'Combined Study and Canteen', Changi.
Sketch by Harry Silman, July 1942

'The Evening Meal', Changi. Sketch by Harry Silman, August 1942

4

My Days Are Settling Down

Changi lies in the north-east of Singapore, which is very close to the equator. It is always hot and humid, with heavy monsoon rains for approximately six months of the year and no real dry season. Today there are wide roads leading to Changi Airport. In the early 1940s the ground was swampy, with exceptionally dense vegetation of palm and rubber trees, making any escape attempt fraught with hazard.

A communiqué with a list of rules and prohibitions was issued by the Japanese High Command on the day following surrender. These included a total ban on all wireless communication and any contact with the outside world. This did not stop the POWs, who listened to illegal radios in secret, enabling them to keep abreast of events in the rest of the Far East and Europe.

The Japanese commander insisted on a full inspection of the prisoners, and made them stand in lines, three deep, along two miles of road for an hour and a half:

26 FEBRUARY 1942

The retinue consisted of a few cars containing camera men who took films for propaganda purposes – very humiliating. We were all glad when the gloating party was over.

The sewage system and water supply had been destroyed, so rectifying these problems took precedence. Sanitary arrangements were non-existent at first. There was a major dysentery epidemic which affected 40 per cent of the prison population within three days of their arrival. At the time there was little understanding among the troops of the fundamental need for hygiene. They had to dig latrines as quickly as possible and build anti-malarial drains. Harry gives a graphic description of the advantages of proper latrines:

16 APRIL 1942

The latrines are now working, but being Indian style it is rather uncomfortable till one gets used to it. Still it is a relief not to have hundreds of bluebottles biting one's bottom, the damp seats, the smell & crowded accommodation of the deep trench type.

Until the engineers got a proper water system going, each man was rationed to two pints of water per person per day for all purposes. This water was from a water cart and not pure; before they could drink it, it had to be chlorinated.

After the shock of finding a convalescing dysentery patient cleaning dixies (large cooking pots) in the cookhouse, Harry took responsibility for disseminating information on the problems of disease, educating the cookhouse workers about the necessity for hygiene and the safe method of cooking rice:

13 MARCH 1942

As part of the blitz against dysentery, all mess tins etc have to be dipped in boiling water and sterilised before and after meals.

He then started a series of lectures to all the troops on dysentery, fly control measures, skin disease, vitamins and general hygiene precautions, using posters to help. He was rather nervous at first, as it had been a long time since he had addressed a gathering, but after the first five minutes he regained his old confidence.

18 APRIL 1942

Fly propaganda is going on nicely, & all men have been lectured, & numerous gruesome placards adorn cookhouses & billets. 25 deaths in the past 4 days is a high mortality rate, and all measures possible must be adopted. Very annoyed with W & Z companies for having lukewarm water for sterilising, after all my efforts. We still meet chaos in some depts

– eg the swill – in spite of the order that swill should be burnt in the incinerator, they sent the stuff back to put on the garden!

He persevered, regardless of these occasional setbacks, and eventually completed lectures to all the companies.

A great improvement several weeks later was the introduction of electric lighting:

3 JUNE 1942

The electric light plant was taken from a large house outside the wire, & brought in by a party of RAOC [Royal Army Ordnance Corps] chaps who fitted it up themselves. They have done an excellent job of work & have a little powerhouse going constantly, either charging batteries or giving us light which is on from 8.15–10.45. The Japs now know about it and have cast covetous eyes on it, so that if they think they may require it, they may whip it all away.

The accommodation in Changi was totally inadequate for the number of troops imprisoned there. They quickly erected bamboo-framed huts covered with canvas, tarpaulins or anything that was suitable. After a short time, part of the 18th Division were allocated to the former India Lines [see Glossary]. They were given two barrack blocks, one for the officers –

Harry's camp identity disc, engraved in English and Japanese

6 MAY 1942

We cleaned up the billet & divided it into three: (i) library (ii) sleeping (iii) ante room; there are several armchairs & tables available & numerous old USA newspapers so that it resembles old times again.

– and the second for senior NCOs. These blocks were originally intended to house 150 but now housed between six and eight hundred.

The junior NCOs and troops were given wooden huts and tents, so everyone had protection from the rain, which was unlike any rainfall they had experienced in Britain. In the monsoon season the rain was torrential, completely drenching clothing and equipment and tearing down trees and wires. However, the rain did have advantages:

24 FEBRUARY 1942

Occasional showers are welcomed as we take off our
clothing and taking a piece of soap, step out into the
rain and give ourselves a good clean up.

Changi had originally been a large British military base,
which had been hastily evacuated on 7 February. It had
suffered from looting by the time it was turned into a POW
camp, but there were many odd materials lying around which
were put to good use. There was much to do to make the billet
habitable:

19 FEBRUARY 1942

By begging, scrounging and borrowing, have
managed to collect a reasonable amount of personal
kit which I have stowed away in my locker and have
borrowed a blanket to cover my sofa-cushion, which
on a table top serves as my bed. Found a camp chair
and a small wooden table so am quite comfortable
for the time being.

The prisoners were short of basic items of clothing and
equipment, and Harry became quite proficient at altering
what he found to suit his current needs. (When they were first
taken into captivity, the prisoners were able to leave the camp
for specific reasons, such as going into Singapore Town to
collect supplies. Later it became much more difficult to do so,
and only authorised people with the relevant documentation

were permitted.) He had overcome his scruples in taking items from deserted homes in Singapore Town, but he noted these in his diaries with the intention of apologising to 'Mr Reeves' after the war.

4 APRIL 1942

List of my Personal Possessions and their former or present owners

Wristlet watch	*Loaned by Archie*
Blanket	*Loaned by Eva*
Pillow case	*Given by Addy*
Shoes	*Borrowed from Mr Reeves*
Topee	*of Singapore (without his*
Towel	*knowledge or permission)*
ARP raincoat	
Hankies	
Blue shorts	
Coloured shirt	*Given by Thornhill*
Short pants	*Taken from some house in Singapore*
2 pairs stockings	*CO's kit left behind*
2 pairs KD shorts	*Taken from Singapore laundry*
2 K shirts	
1 stick	*Converted golf club*
1 forage cap	*Made by me from battle dress trousers of Webb*
1 pair slippers	*Made from old tyres*

1 haversack	*Given by Macreath*
1 spring bed	*Supplied by hospital*
1 long sofa cushion (used as mattress)	*Mr Reeves*
Mosquito net	*'Found'*
1 folding camp chair	*'Found'*
1 table	*'Found'*

In June 1942 the Imperial Japanese Army started to pay the POWs an amenity grant. In the Yorkshire Television documentary *Back to the Front: Doctors at War*, Harry said that the Japanese printed their own banknotes – 'toytown' money. It was not always accepted by the local inhabitants, but it was their only currency.

12 JUNE 1942

> We, in Changi, are very fortunate to get paid as the Japs say that as we do not work, they won't pay us. Personal intervention of the General & the Japs agreed to pay us every 10 days, retrospective from May 1st – $7.50 officers, $4.50 NCOs & $3 for the men.

In this respect, prisoners in Changi were more fortunate than POWs in other Japanese prison camps, who received no pay at all unless they were doing hard labour.

Harry always had a keen sense of the ridiculous:

3 JULY 1942

The amazing part is that the Japs are printing unnumbered notes & giving them to us as an amenity grant, & we are buying the stores which were left behind by the British or were looted from stores. The whole position is ludicrous. It is difficult to ascertain who is making a profit out of these transactions.

The POWs were already buying extra supplies from the local people:

15 MARCH 1942

They are running a very lucrative business selling back to the soldiers all the cigarette and food stores they stole from the barracks. This has to be done surreptitiously as the Japs would shoot both the vendor and emptor if they saw the transactions.

18 MARCH 1942

Prices are going up rapidly as the demand increases and the natives are making a fortune. $5 for jam, $7 for syrup, $3 for bully beef etc. However as my money is no good to me here I am going to spend all I have. Rupees are even being changed at an exorbitant rate.

Their funds enabled them to buy basic necessities.

22 APRIL 1942

More canteen stores have arrived. I just managed to scrape together sufficient money to pay for some shaving cream, a tooth brush, boot polish etc.

They received infrequent supplies from contacts in Singapore Town, who boxed up random items they were able to acquire. Occasionally there was disappointment when the packages were unwrapped:

2 JUNE 1942

When we opened Henry's box from S. which had been packed ready for dispatch for the past 3 months, it was found that the packets of fruit pastilles had melted & mixed with the soap, sugar & toothpaste to form a conglomerate sticky mass. However much of the contents were rescued, but what we are to do with the enormous quantity of soap is not yet decided. I am trying to exchange some of it for bread which an officer is trying to sell.

After about four months they were allowed to send one censored postcard home. Harry was meticulous about following the guidelines, as many of the postcards were returned because the writing was illegible or the senders had broken rules:

20 JUNE 1942

Wrote the postcard home in block letters, being very careful not to include double meanings, Braille etc. Simple childish sentences were the order of the day – I wonder what they will think at home when they see my effort. Still the main thing is to get some sort of message home telling them that I am fit.

Harry practised on a piece of paper before being satisfied he was using his twenty-four words to the best advantage:

I AM A PRISONER OF WAR
I AM SAFE AND WELL
DO NOT WORRY
ALL MY LOVE TO ALL
HOPE YOU ARE ALL WELL.

Although written in uppercase letters, he signed it as normal, so the family would know it had been sent by him.

Harry's postcard home dropped through the letterbox, but unfortunately it slid under a rug and was not found until nearly six months later. It was 17 December (ten months after he was captured) before the family received a telegram confirming that Harry was a prisoner of war. This news was reported on 19 December 1942 in the local paper, *The Yorkshire Post*, under the headline 'NEWS AT LAST OF MISSING MEN: Leeds Officers at Singapore'. The report stated that after months of 'anxious waiting', information about the missing men was now reaching their families: 'Two more Leeds officers … are now

Official telegram informing the Silman family
of Harry's captivity, 17 December 1942

known to be prisoners in the hands of the Japanese. One of them is Captain Harry Silman (32).' In the same newspaper column, there is an article titled: 'EXCELLENT LIFE: Tokyo's Rosy Picture of Prison Camps':

Tokyo radio claimed today that British and Dutch prisoners in Japanese hands were living an excellent and healthy life. 'The place where they are kept is quiet and restful' it was claimed. 'Climate is healthy, surroundings are beautiful and very similar to the Waikiki Beach of Hawaii. Many of the men are devoting a couple of hours every day to the learning of Japanese which is very popular among them all. ... Medical facilities are of the highest order possible, and treatment leaves nothing to be desired. The men are strong and healthy and the authorities are treating them all with due respect.'

One assumes this was intended to reassure the families of the missing men.

Harry occasionally came across people he knew or with whom he shared mutual acquaintances. Maybe the strangest coincidence was the man who was at sick parade one morning.

6 DECEMBER 1942

He told me where I live, & complained about the large postal packets I used to get. He was our postman. What a small world!

Even in this first year there were regular reminders of the cruelty of their captors:

6 JULY 1942

The Japs have chopped off the hands of several Chinese & Malayans & decorating them with ribbons have hung them up in public places as a warning to looters & rioters. This puts the clock back several hundred years.

30 SEPTEMBER 1942

Burn had a bad time to start with, as he was put in a barbed wire cage with no protection against the elements.

There was a constant concern that culture differences could lead to punishment:

5 JULY 1942

Three Jap guards came into the mess during the morning & I had to entertain them with tea & biscuits. Their knowledge of English was confined to Thank you, and we were thanking each other very often. They were amiable, and except for throwing the tea dregs on the floor, behaved very well. They offered me a cigarette & when I refused they started mumbling to each other – I wondered whether I had insulted them.

As with any large organisation, there were sporadic grumbles about those in authority. However, a universally beloved figure was Major-General Beckwith-Smith, who died of heart failure, possibly following diphtheria, after being sent from Changi to Formosa (now Taiwan). He left them on 16 August 1942 and issued a farewell message to the troops:

On my departure for Japan I wish to take what may be my last chance to thank all ranks for their

cheerful, serious and loyal support on many shores
and seas during the two years in which I have had
the honour to command the Division. I regret that I
have been unable to lead you to the success in battle
to which your cause and your sacrifice is entitled
and although I leave you with a heavy heart I carry
with me many precious memories and a sense of real
comradeship such as could only have been inspired
by the trials and disappointments which we have
shared in the last few months.

Harry said the news of Becky's death was a terrible blow to
everyone in the 18th Division as he was very much respected
and loved:

22 NOVEMBER 1942

We all hoped that when we got back to England, he
would act as our spokesman & explain the raw deal
that our Div got in this battle.

Even the local Japanese propaganda newspaper, *The Syonan
Times*, gave a front-page column to his death, describing
the homage that was paid to him by Japanese and Allied
commanders alike as he lay in state.

5

The Food Question Is Rather Important

Food was a major concern, and meals were eagerly anticipated, not just because the men were desperately hungry but also to break up the monotony of the day. It is understandable that Harry frequently writes about food in his diaries. After a few months he said he was getting used to the short rations and had lost that continual sense of slight hunger, but he was definitely below par in general fitness.

To begin with, the meals consisted almost entirely of their army rations of bully beef (tinned corn beef) and hardtack biscuits (a type of cracker):

23 FEBRUARY 1942

The food is causing many grumbles as the midday meal consists of tea and three biscuits and there is nothing till 6.30 when we partake of a bully beef stew and more tea and biscuits.

20 MARCH 1942

Tea is served without milk or sugar – soon it will be without tea. The milk and sugar rations one supposes go into making the other foods.

The staple food was rice, and in some of the early days, this was virtually all they had:

5 MARCH 1942

The food question is rather important. We are getting almost ¾ lb of rice a day in various forms but mostly boiled – sometimes curried and sometimes with stew. Some of the meals consist of sugarless tea and tasteless rice – causing discontent. The cooks are being changed in the hope of getting tastier meals. There is too much eyeing the other fellows' rations and the complaints about other units getting more or better rations are numerous and groundless. There is a mad scramble after the meals have been issued for the small quantity left over in the dixies. It amazes me how the men can consume such large quantities of rice by itself. They can't possibly be hungry after a meal. I'm full of rice but the chaps come back for more.

After a new messing officer was appointed the food started to improve and there were fewer complaints.

'*Queuing for food.*' *Sketch by the Dutch artist and POW Henk Brouwer*

Whenever the Japanese wanted to punish the prisoners, the food was restricted to just rice:

9 APRIL 1942

A soldier from Southern Command was found outside the wire two nights ago and was shot by the Japs. They have punished us all by stopping our next meat, cigarette and soap ration. We will have to live almost on rice alone for the next week.

The cooks became quite inventive with methods of using rice. The very popular breakfast porridge was made with ground rice and sweetened with diluted condensed milk. Harry said he felt comfortable and happy after breakfast, which would set him up for the day. His batman roasted some rice grains that Harry ground into a powder and stirred into boiling water. He declared it tasted like good coffee.

They were able to get supplies of meat from Singapore Town but had occasional problems:

8 APRIL 1942

The large supply of fresh meat went bad today and we will have two meatless days. It was sheer stupidity keeping that meat in lukewarm water overnight. We have to be very careful of every morsel of protein and vitamin ... Half the meat supply to the camp was condemned as being bad – this was due to the refrigerator in Singapore going off. The meat should have been used up quickly – it was a heart-breaking sight to see all the carcasses being buried and men eating plain rice. The diet is bound to have an effect on the general health and teeth in the long run.

The prisoners also kept chickens and ducks with varying degrees of success:

27 MARCH 1942

The officers' mess bought 20 chickens locally and are keeping them in a hastily erected hen run at the back. They look rather small so that it will be months before we get an egg for breakfast.

Then, two days later:

Chickens bought for the mess are dying off rapidly maybe due to croup. It is possible that the Malayans, finding the disease spreading among a brood, sell the seemingly healthy ones off cheaply and after the incubation period of the disease the birds die.

The hens did provide eggs for breakfast, although they had to wait between two and four months for their turn. They could also buy eggs from the Local Purchase Canteen, but they were in short supply. Eggs were one of the dishes Harry really missed.

However, they sometimes had quite surprisingly good meals considering their incarceration.

5 JULY 1942

The combined efforts of the MOs caused the deaths of ten of the ducks for dinner tonight – a good portion for each officer with roast potatoes, veg & stuffing, followed by a doughnut & cream!

The POWs were resourceful in their quest for food. Stray animals were caught – Harry said stray dogs would enter the cookhouse at their peril. One evening the Japanese sent a large quantity of assorted fish, including catfish, dogfish, eels and shark. Harry said that most of it was already going bad, but the rest was gutted by the light of the moon and covered over till the morning. There is no record in the diary of any meal with this fish, apart from the fact that there was an outbreak of diarrhoea the next day.

Desserts were not forgotten. Fertiliser was used to make a sweet course, apparently full of vitamins. Bananas and pineapples were plentiful and cheap on the island, and they had a regular delivery of pineapples to the mess.

10 JUNE 1942

Unfortunately after they have been peeled & the cooks have had their rake-off, there isn't very much left to go on the 'pineapple flan'.

They also bought seeds and grew crops. They had flourishing gardens that provided quite a few vegetable and salad items, which were vital in supplementing their vitamin-poor diet. Harry managed to find a book about vegetable gardening in Malaya and learned that a local crop, *kangkong* (water spinach), contains large amounts of vitamin A as well as iron. In addition, he found that peanuts are a good source not just of fat and protein but also vitamins B and C, so that the two together were an excellent combination from a nutritional viewpoint. However, he noted on 17 June,

> the leaves which form our veg are almost tasteless and it is like eating grass. The absence of salt is felt, especially in the veg.

Harry and his friends made the most of any opportunity to acquire food. There are several diary entries when it is evident they ate well if not wisely:

10 APRIL 1942

> At night shared my bully with Carter's bread. 3 of us had a good tuck-in. Then the padre felt hungry so opened and shared a tin of herrings with him. An RASC [Royal Army Service Corps] officer brought in some yam and some mouldy Indian biscuits so there was quite a party.

30 APRIL 1942

Terrific party full of vitamins – tomato juice, pilchards, salmon, with bread, marg & marmalade-sweetened orange juice & a tin of pineapple each.

14 JULY 1942

We have a small petrol stove in the billet, and at night we fry minced up sardines & rice or fried bread (when we get any). It makes a tasty dish with Soya sauce added.

21 APRIL 1942

Had a party at night in Padre's room – herrings, bread, biscuits & jam, & then followed it up with one in mine – bully & rice & marmalade. Felt rather sick.

These evening 'parties' were clearly the highlight of the day. They were social occasions when they talked well into the night discussing the latest rumours about the war and diverse topics including politics, religion and philosophy. Harry frequently said he went to bed feeling very full and contented.

He also experimented with making interesting brews:

15 MAY 1942

I am making a potent alcoholic drink, ostensibly for its vitamin B content, but raisins, sugar & pineapple juice, if allowed to stand for a few days, make a drink containing more than vit B. These yeast drinks form a very interesting experiment, and consequently more research is required.

He originally concocted it for the Padre's birthday.

17 MAY 1942

'Silman's Special' was the hard drink, & a mighty fine brew it was – I must try it when I get home.

Later in the year he experimented further to make the brew more potent, and he renamed it Panther's Breath.

They occasionally got Red Cross parcels with precious food items, including much-prized Marmite, but after the Japanese surrendered at the end of the war, it was found that they had kept a very large proportion of the Red Cross parcels for themselves. Nonetheless, these early entries certainly give the impression that conditions in Changi were reasonably satisfactory for a POW camp.

After half a year's incarceration, Harry noted that he had gradually become acclimatised:

22 AUGUST 1942

1. I rarely get up during the night now.
2. I never perspire at night – at first I used to wake up wringing with sweat.

3. I use a hankie a day now and at first a hankie would last me a week.
4. I rarely drink any water now during the day.
5. I feel more active and lively as distinct from that heavy lethargic feeling we first had.
6. I've lost that constant state of hunger that I originally had, and made some people into animals.

16 AUGUST 1942

It is now six months since the capitulation – half a year of captivity which on looking back has passed very quickly and not too uncomfortably. Originally we thought that conditions and food would rapidly deteriorate but on the contrary the food and rations have improved and we can buy almost anything we like from the canteen.

But the Japanese never let them forget they were prisoners. In the same entry on 28 May, where Harry had written

Special menu in evening for overseas party only – duck & green peas. They had a dinner worthy of the Grosvenor. It is a strange POW camp that allows us to turn out such a magnificent repast.

he also noted:

We heard that the C-in-C [commander in chief] has been kept in a cell for 4 days without food – no comforts or furniture – & was questioned & requestioned in the hope that his resistance would break down. The Japs go to both extremes, and one can never be certain whether one will be treated very kindly or biffed over the head with a rifle.

6

I Had the Largest Sick Parade Ever

On 18 February 1942 Harry's RAP was held on the grass, and he and his medical orderlies were working from morning till night tending the sick and wounded. Two days later they moved into a small concrete hut, which was much cooler. Harry had daily sick parades with two teams of orderlies so they could run morning and afternoon sessions. He sympathised with the large queue of sodden soldiers lining up in the pouring rain, patiently waiting for dressings. However, on 16 March he noted the advantage to the early morning starts as he was given one of the things he missed most:

> a really good cup of tea with plenty of milk and sugar
> in it – not like the watery unsweetened stuff that they
> put on the table for meal times.

Occasionally they did not have enough hours in the day to see everyone individually:

9 SEPTEMBER 1942

On Monday afternoon I had the largest sick parade
ever. 186 men attending for examination and
treatment. I took them in bundles of 10 and was a
limp rag when I had finished.

At these sick parades he saw frequent occurrences of diseases
which he had previously only come across in textbooks.
He managed to find a tome on tropical diseases, which
was helpful in adding to the practical knowledge he was
gaining on a daily basis. Harry welcomed the opportunity to
discuss worrying cases with the other medics in the regular
meetings of the Changi Medical Society when the British
and Australian doctors shared their findings and confirmed
statistics of specific diseases and the deaths arising. Much
of their clinical treatment was based on trial and error,
especially as they were so short of the drugs that were
needed to effect cures.

Beriberi, a disease that afflicted a very high proportion
of the POWs and caused many deaths, was a major topic of
discussion. Harry knew that vitamin B in rice is dissolved out
by washing and was their main source of the vitamin in the
prison diet. There was an order that rice was not to be washed
but cooked once in its own water till it was all evaporated, but
he admitted that this caused difficulties owing to lack of time,
fuel and cooking space. He spent much time encouraging the
men to eat rice polishings (RPs), a good source of the vitamin,
so as to combat beriberi and other vitamin-deficiency diseases
that were becoming a major problem. Jim Bradley, in *Towards*

the Setting Sun, said they found the rice polishings almost unpalatable:

> I think no-one would have attempted to take these, had we not all been so afraid of becoming impotent! The only way to get them down was to put them in a mug, add water, and as they were completely insoluble, swill them down; these rice polishings were nauseating and alive with weevils.

Allied prisoners of war in Southeast Asia suffering from beriberi

The medics did not discourage them from eating the weevils in the food, as they were a source of protein, however small.

Harry also suspected that a lack of vitamin B was only part of the picture, as some developed beriberi on a good mixed diet while others on a poor diet did not. There was agreement that deficiency of all the vitamins was bound to complicate the picture, because there was no factor common to every case. The message about the value of vitamins was obviously conveyed well to the troops. Padre Cordingly commented that 'soon the whole camp was discussing Vitamins as though they were some new delicacy we should seek'.

This is one of numerous diary entries chronicling Harry's concern with their poor diet:

23 SEPTEMBER 1942

The position in regard to vitamins is very serious. About a third of the Battalion is suffering from one form or another of deficiency ... I now hear that the so-called Rice Polishings consists of floor sweepings & is not true polishings, containing no B2 and is therefore useless for treatment. If this is the case we are foxed as there are no other remedies to use. The outlook is very grave unless the Japs will provide a good source of B2 for us. One RAOC man developed complete paralysis of his legs in 24 hours – motor & sensory. How little do people in England realise the importance of vitamins in the diet. I called a meeting of the two messing officers &

discussed future policy. A memo came out recently stating minimum amounts of peanuts, RP, palm oil & whitebait to be included in the daily diet.

There were other diseases that the doctors also ascribed to vitamin deficiency in their diet, including encephalitis, sprue, pellagra, scrotal dermatitis and stomatitis. Marmite helped to combat some of these conditions but was in woefully short supply.

Harry said it took a little while before they diagnosed an eye condition caused by vitamin A deficiency. It started off with pain and blurring of vision, and if not diagnosed in time it caused permanent blindness. He also wondered if conjunctivitis, which was similarly prevalent, might be connected to a vitamin A deficiency.

A real headache for Harry was the number of men with metatarsalgia – acutely painful feet. He was baffled by the fact that they did not show much improvement after a week of large doses of rice polishings, as it was thought the condition was caused by lack of vitamin B. He found it strange that the condition seemed to be more painful when the patients were in bed, and he had many discussions with colleagues on the search for a cause and treatment, hoping to do something to relieve the pain and the insomnia it caused.

Another major problem was malaria. The Medical Society gave two lectures on malaria, which Harry said were very interesting, with much new material:

9 SEPTEMBER 1942

Malaria cases when discharged are now divided into two groups A and B. A are in good condition and would live through another attack, B are in bad condition and may get a deficiency disease and sink after another attack. This latter group will have atebrin twice weekly to ward off attacks.

Harry himself had recurrent attacks of malaria for several years after he was liberated, probably in common with many ex-POWs.

He was upset that there was little he could do in cases which would not have been fatal under normal circumstances:

30 AUGUST 1942

Scrotal dermatitis caused 2 deaths last week – some cases are very bad and the men roll about in agony on their beds. Marmite seems to help some cases. There is a vast field of research here.

A dysentery epidemic had started within the first few days of arrival in Changi, and it continued to be a constant cause for concern. A virulent form came in from Singapore, and the early poor sanitary conditions and lack of hygiene among the troops contributed to the increase of the infection. It was so common that Harry said it was easy to overlook symptoms of other conditions:

6 APRIL 1942

Although not on duty I saw three cases in the evening, including a query appendicitis which I sent to hospital late at night. It is very difficult to distinguish between the abdominal pain of dysentery and a true appendicitis and one must be careful not to miss the latter.

There was news of an outbreak of cholera in Singapore.

27 JUNE 1942

I took immediate steps to see that all water, vegetables & fruit are boiled. I hope it doesn't spread up to Changi otherwise we are all in a helluva mess. No word of prophylactic inoculation – I doubt whether there is sufficient supply on the island.

In fact, the cholera scare was caused by one case on board a ship coming into Singapore. The man was quarantined, and all emergency measures, including inoculation, were temporarily suspended. However, the authorities took the situation seriously and issued instructions about observing strict sanitation. Cholera inoculations were given to the cooks and anyone who handled food, plus all the medical officers. Usually the reaction is slight, but Harry developed a fever after his injection. Vaccine was provided by the Japanese for a second cholera inoculation on 11 July, although it looked to Harry like a 'clear water coloured fluid. As I have had no reaction at all, I suspect it may actually be water.' Harry's misgivings may have been well-founded, as the vaccinations seemed to give little protection less than a year later when they were sent up country.

Cases of diphtheria increased as the incarceration continued, and the hospital wards set aside for these patients soon filled up. It began with the arrival of new POWs who were not isolated. Harry thought it careless that they were allowed to mix and sleep alongside all the other internees. He said that the fatal nature of diphtheria was apt to be forgotten and that the MOs who sat on cases of suspected tonsillitis were endangering the lives of men. The shortage of antitoxin and bacteriological facilities were severe drawbacks.

There was a wide variety of work for the medics. Harry recounted one of his disagreeable tasks:

27 MAY 1942

Examined the feet & between the toes of the men, looking for Singapore foot (not a pleasant pastime esp. after lunch – rather malodorous). Found about 25 new cases – rather a large proportion in our small community – largely due to shower baths & men walking about in bare feet. This is now strictly forbidden.

One job he did not enjoy was collecting smears for medical examination:

9 FEBRUARY 1943

It was my fate last Sat. to be a sticker i.e. for 2 hours I was inserting glass rods into large bottoms pushed into my face, obscuring all other views. The whole proceedings were very unpleasant, and the sight of the colonels and officers with their trousers down was rather humiliating. Everyone took it in good part and joked about it for several days afterwards. I was the butt of numerous jokes.

Harry's medical notes contained the occasional unusual report:

3 JULY 1942

A fusilier vomited up a roundworm 8" long – he says it gave him a shock! Worms are an oft unsuspected cause of abdominal pain, nausea, vomiting & possibly loss of weight. Worms are quite common in this country.

At regular periods prisoners were sent from Changi to Japan. Before they went the medics had to do rigorous inspections, taking blood samples and smears for examination:

20 JULY 1942

The organisation necessary to prepare, number & examine all the specimens is enormous. Besides this, all the luggage will be put through a disinfectant to 60°. Personal kit carried in a pack will be sprayed with carbolic & the person himself will be dipped in disinfectant. They are certainly sparing no effort to make sure that we take no disease into Japan. What amazed me was to see a small Jap MO standing on tiptoe to prick the ears of the tall British Tommies.

Not surprisingly, the medical officers themselves were not immune from illness. Harry had a severe attack of dengue, a tropical disease spread by mosquitoes. Unlike most of his patients he was ill for ten days:

31 JULY 1942

During the dengue do, the other lads were very attentive & scrambled eggs for me & once the Padre cut it up small & kneeling down by my bed, he fed me like a child.

When he started to feel like eating again, well-meaning friends shared a half-tin of sardines, opened the previous day, which unfortunately led to severe gastroenteritis for Harry and two companions. Severely dehydrated, they were sent in an ambulance to hospital. In the same entry, Harry related:

There was much consternation amongst the officers and spectators who saw us being taken away as we looked almost moribund. After a wait of ¾ hour in the reception office, we were carried up 3 flights of stairs by four non-co-operative stretcher bearers & my life was in danger of being suddenly ended. Fortunately the attack very soon settled down.

A couple of incidents at sick parade caused Harry some amusement:

25 FEBRUARY 1943

I said to one group of fellows who turned up for inoculation 'Are you 2nd dysenteries?' They said 'No, 1st Cambridgeshires'! One American seaman was put down as 'Dennis' on the sick report. When he came in he said his name wasn't Dennis but Atlopozcyki (or something similar) – he had toothache and he wanted to see a 'dennis'.

Harry's medical duties in Changi, although at times quite demanding, seemed very straightforward when he looked back from the horrendous conditions he would find when he was up country in Thailand.

7

Men Have Turned to Religion for Mental Comfort

The Japanese were quite happy for the POWs to follow their religious customs. Indeed, they actively encouraged religious life, perhaps because they respected religion and many were very superstitious, but it also kept the prisoners occupied. Even when privileges and food were withdrawn, religious buildings and services were not affected.

Harry was very friendly with the Padre. They were both attached to the regiment but classified differently from the regular soldiers, and they were both fully occupied in their respective positions. Each appreciated the other's role. A few years ago I was given information enabling me to contact the Padre's daughter, Louise Reynolds, and I learned that her father equally valued his friendship with Harry. Louise kindly sent me a copy of her father's diaries, and her research into his memoirs gave me an insight into his work.

Within twenty-four hours of being taken prisoner Padre

Eric Cordingly found a little mosque, once used for Indian troops who used to live in the area, and knew that it would be well suited as a church, as it was light and cool. By the end of the week skilled volunteers had lovingly made a pulpit and altar and produced seating and furnishings. They repurposed tin tubes to resemble candles that held small tin cups for an oil/paraffin mix. When lit, he said they were hardly distinguishable from the real thing. Later a beautiful brass cross was fashioned from a howitzer shell case, and this cross was taken from camp to camp as the prisoners were moved. When the war ended the Padre took the cross back home to the UK, and in 1992 the family donated it to the Changi Chapel.

'St George's Chapel' in a converted mosque, Changi.
Watercolour by Lt E. Stacy RE

The Padre's Sunday services were very well attended, as were various discussion groups during the week, finishing with a simple service at the end of each day. Eric Cordingly said that for him it was 'a wonderful time in my life in spite of the grim times'. A large proportion of the men appreciated the spiritual consolation offered by the regular services, and he wrote in his diaries that he never felt more needed:

> It must be obvious that in our present circumstances as prisoners of war, the work of a padre can be tremendous, his scope is as never before in his life, his opportunities are enormous ... Gone temporarily is the rush and hurry and noise of a working, fighting world, and away in a quiet corner of the world, men are inevitably taking stock of themselves.
>
> The Church was packed for Evensong last night, and half an hour before the service it was impossible to get a seat ... All the officers who come bring their own chairs with them. It is an amusing sight to watch men approaching from all directions, carrying chairs of all sorts and descriptions.

Easter and Christmas services were especially meaningful. The first Easter in captivity was 'an amazing revelation'. The church was decorated with beautiful white, sweet-smelling frangipani, and the Padre noted:

> I felt somehow that here in our regular life away from the rush and bustle of the world outside, we

had captured the atmosphere of the week. Good Friday and Easter Day stood out so clearly in our life here.

The religious aspect of Christmas was celebrated with a short service on Christmas Eve, a midnight Eucharist, a pre-dawn service on Christmas Day and concluded with a carol service: 'Peace on earth to men of goodwill, that was the prayer on each person's mind.'

Padre Cordingly kept an accurate account of all the funerals he had organised, and after he was repatriated he spent many months writing to the families of the prisoners he had cared for before they died.

Harry was from an Orthodox Jewish family and, although not very observant himself, he very quickly identified a need to have weekly Shabbat (Sabbath) services and keep, as far as possible, the age-old traditions of the festivals. It is interesting that, although in Japanese eyes all prisoners were the lowest of the low, there was virtually no incidence of anti-Semitism. There was some concern when a nominal roll of all Jewish personnel was requested, as many men thought it might lead to a similar situation as in Europe, but it was purely for record purposes. Harry learned that the proportion of Jews in the army was 0.5 per cent, which was much higher than he thought. He was able to find people in different areas who would take responsibility for Jewish burial services if necessary.

Harry was somewhat surprised to find that initially he became the spokesman for the Jewish prisoners as the majority were non-practising. He organised the first of what would be regular Friday night services in Changi. To start with, these were held wherever they could find a suitable venue:

27 FEBRUARY 1942

Attended my first army religious service – strange that it should be as a prisoner of war. I was the only officer, 1 Sergeant, 1 Corporal and about 16 ORs. No-one had a prayer book so we had a short stand up service – three men each reciting a bit of a prayer that they could remember. The service was held at 8 PM in a rubber plantation behind some distant billets. We couldn't sit down owing to the ants.

As they had no prayer books at the time, Harry arranged for certain men to write out the prayers they could remember for the following week, hoping they could have a more satisfactory service. This was held in a small sports pavilion out in the woods:

6 MARCH 1942

It started in a typical fashion 30 minutes late – one man had a *siddur* [prayer book] and acted as *chazan* [cantor who leads the congregation] so that we had a fairly good service. Two men with good voices acted as the nucleus of a choir and led the singing. After such absence from services it will take a little while before the words become familiar again.

It took a couple of weeks before they could find a more suitable venue for their service. Harry was greatly relieved when the senior padre called in on him in the MI room and offered his little church near Division HQ for the Friday night services – 'a very decent gesture'.

Attendance improved greatly over time at the weekly services, although Harry was rather disappointed that only a few of the Jewish officers turned up, even though there seemed to be an increasing trend towards religion:

27 JUNE 1942

It is strange how men have turned to religion for mental comfort while a POW. The Padre has services morning & night, & crowded services on Sunday. It gives a certain feeling of relief & satisfaction to lift up one's voice in hymns etc. It is a pity we haven't sufficient prayer books & a good *chazan* so that we could do that.

Over the three and a half years of captivity, services became more refined. David Arkush, a dentist, was also from an Orthodox Jewish family, and his father was a *chazan*. He joined the small congregation soon after the start. He had brought his prayer book with him and made a highly valued contribution to the services before he was sent away:

1 APRIL 1942

Capt Arkush of ADC gave them a short talk afterwards about Jewish life in Singapore. He hopes to give them similar talks after each service. It is a good idea and helps them to remember their faith and upbringing.

The first day of Rosh Hashanah, the Jewish New Year, had a record attendance:

15 SEPTEMBER 1942

Owing to the limitations imposed by the prayer book it is difficult to give a true service but we managed to put bits and pieces together and all in all, it worked out very well.

Ten days later was Yom Kippur, the Day of Atonement, and normally a fast day. Harry thought there would not be many who would fast this year, and he himself would not encourage it under the circumstances, leaving it to each man's choice. This High Holy Day service meant a lot to him:

22 SEPTEMBER 1942

Yesterday was the most remarkable Yom Kippur I have ever spent. We had two services, a long morning one and a shorter afternoon one. There were over 70 present in the morning including a few

RAF newly arrived. Capt. Phillips had prepared an anglicised service. We read a portion about Isaac in English. One of the men asked us if we could finish by 12.30 as they had to back for 1 o'clock for dinner! A few observed the day strictly, but those that didn't can be forgiven for it was terrifically hot & sweat was pouring out of us as we stood listening.

Over the years in Changi services were held in a variety of venues including the Sergeants' Mess and a cinema in the hospital grounds. It was not until a year before they were liberated that a small synagogue, Ohel Jacob, was built in the prison camp.

Ohel Jacob, the prison camp synagogue. Sketch by George Sprod

In January 1943 a Dutch rabbi from Indonesia, Rabbi Chaim Nussbaum, came into the camp. He conducted services and kept a record of the festivals which were celebrated as best they could, sometimes with a considerable amount of ingenuity:

30 MARCH 1945

2 nights ago I attended a Seder service [special prayers and meal for the festival of Pesach/Passover] – a remarkably successful affair. Nussbaum is a genius for overcoming difficulties. We had matzo made out of sago flour, wine made from fermented rice water. The four cups consisted of coffee owing to the shortage of wine. Charoseth was grated coconut and sugar, maror was mint leaves, and for hard-boiled eggs we had spinach leaves. Somehow Pesach doesn't seem the same without hard-boiled eggs. However it all made me feel quite homesick and over coffee and smokes at the end, we sang the usual songs and broke up after a very merry evening.

Rabbi Nussbaum gave Harry a *siddur*, which he treasured greatly and brought back from the war.

Whenever Harry wrote about the festivals, it is clear his thoughts turned to home:

1 APRIL 1942

As I walked to the service I thought of everyone at home and felt sure that they would at the same time be thinking about me and under what circumstances I was living. It is at times like this that one thinks of one's family & vice versa.

8

Idleness Is a Curse

When the troops were taken prisoner, apart from those with specific roles – the padres, doctors, engineers, cooks, etc. – there was very little to occupy their time. Harry felt he was lucky, as he had his work as a Medical Officer that filled a large part of his day:

24 FEBRUARY 1942

My days are settling down to a definite routine of work and most of my time is occupied. The other officers and men find that time hangs heavily on their hands – this accounts for the numerous complaints about food and other things. Idleness is a curse and is one of the worst features of the POW camp. It gives men too much time to sit and think and brood. I am only too glad to get into a chair or bed to rest after a long session in the MI Room.

Maintaining the morale of the prisoners in Changi was essential. The most popular highlights were the frequent concert parties and shows. Harry describes one show which ended with a full orchestra on the stage, including a xylophone. With such a huge prison population there was a wealth of talent, not only in musicians, actors, singers and variety acts but also with people who had backstage skills in lighting, sound and set design.

One of the captives in Changi was Ronald Searle. Although best known later for his cartoons and caricatures, he was responsible for the programme design and professional scenery for many of the shows. After the war he published a graphic pictorial account of the horrors endured by POWs in the Far East.

Harry enjoyed every production he saw. These included *The Dover Road*, *The Dancing Years* and *Badger's Green*, a play about village life that had been successful in London. He was held spellbound by the dramatic last scene in *The Monkey's Paw*, even though he had seen it before, and he rated each show very highly, commenting on the excellent scenery and costumes. On 17 September 1942, after the opening night of *I Killed the Count*, he commented that

> the scenery and decor could not have been better even in a London show. The Sappers made the scenery and converted old furniture into modern stuff. The acting was of a very high standard. Wilkie, the star performer as the Chief Inspector had a very long part to learn and was word perfect. They have

been unfortunately stricken with illness and each day some member of the cast gets ill and they have to rehearse it all over again with the new addition. This must be very tiring.

Harry, with friends from the 18th Division, went over to a different section to see George Bernard Shaw's play *Arms and the Man*.

31 MAY 1942

It was an open air show in a grassy hollow with scenery made out of twigs & leaves – very ingeniously constructed portions fixed into slots in the ground. The actors had a remarkable variety of makeshift uniforms & dresses. Although the play was written 40 years ago, many passages were strangely topical & could have been applied to the Jap–British fight. Five minutes before the end it started to pour down, so that the play ended prematurely & in some disorder.

Each group was allocated a specific day to see the Division concert, and Harry's group had to accept untimely endings quite frequently because of the weather. One of these shows was aptly named *Rain or Shine*.

On another occasion he managed to get a seat in the front row:

3 NOVEMBER 1942

The compere, with a serious face, announced during the show 'Is there a doctor in the house?' I knew the old joke but as I was pointed out he asked me 'How do you like the show Doc?' There was a tremendous burst of laughter and cheering, and now everywhere I go I am greeted with that phrase. The compere told some of the dirtiest jokes I have ever heard in my life. The men enjoyed them but the colonels were very annoyed.

Some of the performers went on to become renowned in show business after they were released. Sydney Piddington was a 'thought reader' who had a very popular act to entertain the troops. After the war he and his wife performed as The Piddingtons, and were world-famous for their telepathy act.

Harry went to a couple of clairvoyant acts but was very sceptical:

28 NOVEMBER 1942

Last night the Dutch thought-reader made a return visit. I bet the Padre 20 cigs beforehand that it was all a fake & was done by using an accomplice in the room. I decided on a test & gave sealed instructions to Doc Emery who was acting as the medium, so that only Emery & myself knew what he had to do. After a lot of fumbling, he performed the task written down. This completely shattered my disbelief

& scepticism. With my scientific education, I have hitherto refused to believe anything supernatural, anything that could not be explained by ordinary laws of physics, chemistry, etc. The existence of God came into the argument with the Padre, who argued that just because he couldn't prove scientifically the presence of a God, it doesn't mean to say that there isn't one. The experiment last night shows that there are still lots of phenomena that cannot be explained in our present state of knowledge & there may be something in spiritualism etc.

Harry also attended a demonstration of hypnotism:

16 MARCH 1943

A young medical orderly was hypnotised after only 30 seconds and was kept under for 30 minutes. He was as stiff as a log and was suspended between two chairs, and a heavy man jumped on his middle without bending him. I examined the boy while he was under the influence and was much impressed. He was in a state of tonic contraction, (except his arms which were flaccid), his pupils were fixed and dilated – insensitive to pain – P and R [pulse and respiration] normal. He came round quite easily and except for feeling very tired there were no after effects. He described a sensation as of electric shocks going through him and he was helpless and unable to move. He then remembered nothing till he woke up. This demonstration of Hypnotism and the previous one of Thought-Reading, both by Dutchmen, have made me a believer in the occult. I am now willing to believe anything!

Among the popular performers were the female impersonators. Gloria d'Earie had been a well-known drag act before the war:

1 JULY 1942

She was more feminine than a girl. The Apache dance was a perfect one & 'she' was always graceful & light. She talked, sang & danced like a girl.

There were several entertainers who were very willing to dress as women, including a successful Australian performer who was known as 'Judy' (as in Garland). They managed to obtain make-up left behind by nurses when they evacuated the island, and when this ran out the chemists were able to manufacture substitutes. Some shows would end with the 'lady' lifting up his skirt to reveal his male credentials. Apparently some of the female impersonators were so convincing the Japanese guards would dash backstage to check for themselves that no women had been smuggled into the camp.

The performers were careful to omit specific sections overtly critical of the Japanese, if they saw they were attending the concerts. As a general rule the material in the shows was not censored in advance, apart from banning the singing of the national anthem, which the Japanese thought would encourage demonstrations of patriotism. So, instead, the producers of the shows substituted 'Land of Hope and Glory'.

Sport flourished in Changi. There were several elite sportsmen among the prisoners who hoped to revive their careers at the end of the war, and they organised football, rugby, hockey, cricket, baseball and basketball matches. Watching the American seamen playing baseball, Harry said that hearing the US twang and expressions was just like a scene in a film. There was always some game to watch:

7 JUNE 1942

The officers played the NCOs [non-commissioned officers] at football – the former seemed to spend most of their time on the ground. Some of them had sticking plaster on various parts of their anatomies in the evening.

There was a degree of rivalry between the Australian and British POWs, and Harry enjoyed watching an Aussies-versus-British cricket match:

10 MAY 1942

They scored over 200 for 4 declared and we were all out for 60. It was amazing to see in a POW camp, spectators sitting around in long cane chairs, some with sunshades, and watching 'Test cricket'.

Harry was mainly an observer rather than a participant in sporting events. However, he took golf lessons from a fellow POW who had been an assistant pro before the war.

6 DECEMBER 1942

I can now hit a reasonable straight drive. How long I can do this is a matter of speculation.

The golf instruction came in useful, as Harry continued to be a keen golfer well into his late seventies.

The prisoners organised a 'race meeting':

4 FEBRUARY 1943

Last Sat. night, the first Changi Spring Meeting was held on the Padang in front of our mess. The RE made a Tote which was illuminated, likewise the course. The horses were men with a wooden horse fore and aft, and the whole affair passed off very successfully. There was the usual excitement and feverish betting – in fact one quite forgot that this is a POW camp. I, being broke, borrowed a few cents and backed all the losers. It was a good thing that I didn't have much money to play with.

To begin with, they were allowed to go swimming on Changi beach. It involved climbing over barbed wire and negotiating patches of oil, but it was a very welcome respite from the monotony of camp life. The Japanese stopped this for a time but later reinstated the privilege:

19 MAY 1942

First bathing party for many months. It was a long walk about 2 miles – not very pleasant water, rather dirty & barbed wire on concealed bottom step made it a dangerous business. I cut my knees & legs in a few places. Still it was a good change & I got a little exercise out of it.

The POWs were quite ingenious in making the best of the materials to hand. One day, early in captivity, Harry spent the afternoon making himself a pair of slippers from an old tyre, which was an arduous task as he had to cut through the thick rubber. Three days later he started to make himself a cap from a borrowed pair of battledress trousers. This was also hard work and took him a few days. When he wore it for the first time he was very relieved there were no caustic comments, unlike the time he decided to try to grow a moustache. He said he had thoughts of Errol Flynn as he cultivated it:

18 OCTOBER 1942

As day succeeded day, it looked more like a rat-bitten toothbrush so this morning it came off mid much wailing and moaning.

Many afternoons Harry was free from medical duties, so he would change into his blue shorts and homemade slippers and potter about doing odd jobs until about 6 o'clock, when he had a shower in time for dinner. He had no problem filling his time.

1 JULY 1942

> I have started drawing in fine perspective style my portion of the billet – it will always be engraved on my mind, but the drawing [see page 36] will help.

He said there was general praise when he completed this, his first drawing since he left school, and it 'exceeded my most sanguine expectations'. Learning to touch-type was another way of passing the occasional hour.

Harry had a number of diary entries detailing his vain efforts at finding the definitive fly paper to solve the perennial fly problem:

10 MARCH 1942

> In PM carried on with my fly-paper experiments – very enjoyable as it involves cutting up (and eating) coconuts …

11 MARCH 1942

> Most of my furniture is very sticky following my experiments on fly catching fluids. Am using various

combinations of castor oil, coconut oil, cachou nut resin and the scummy stuff from the Jack-fruit tree. No success so far.

A very popular institution was what was known as the 'Changi University'. Officers gave lectures on their specialist subjects, and there was a good variety on offer including economics, law, maths, theology and several languages.

14 APRIL 1942

The lectures are now in full swing & the whole place has a studious atmosphere with the fellows walking about with books & pads under their arms. Even the General is attending the theology lectures.

Harry chose to study German, mainly because it did not clash with his sick parades. He took it seriously, practising sometimes for four to five hours in his spare time. Books in modern languages were scarce, so he borrowed a German grammar book and copied it out in full. Even before the university classes started, he had been studying from a teach-yourself German book. He was introduced to a young Swiss man by the Padre and arranged to spend an hour each day with him for conversation. He felt he had mastered sufficient knowledge to keep German conversation going and clearly had achieved quite a reasonable standard, as he was able to read a couple of books in German with the aid of a dictionary.

Harry also studied Italian and was very pleased he could

converse with his Italian patients, who, he wrote, came to him
with the most obscure complaints. It is clear Harry enjoyed
studying languages, as he talked about learning Russian from
native speakers in the camp and basic Japanese from a self-
teaching handbook. He kept up with his schoolboy French by
reading some simple French books that were available.

The POWs had pooled their books to form an eclectic
library, and Harry spent much spare time reading a wide
variety of fiction and non-fiction. These included medical
tomes, Churchill's speeches in Hansard and novels by many
authors, including A. A. Milne, P. G. Wodehouse, Marguerite
Steen and Sapper's *Bulldog Drummond* books. He read
Haldane's *Science in Peace and War*.

17 MAY 1942

I don't like the way he mixes science & Socialism.
Everything that's new, good or progressive he
attributes to Lenin, Marx & USSR, and anything
vaguely bad or wrong he blames Tories, Chamberlain
or Capitalists. It is remarkable for a man to use
politics as examples in a scientific book.

During the first few weeks in Changi, he found it quite hard
to concentrate on reading for long periods and said that other
people had the same difficulty. He gradually adjusted to
prison life:

9 JUNE 1942

I am improving the shining hour by delving deep into
the library – mainly English literature, geography &
history. I am rather pleased with myself that I can
now sit down & enjoy a book that I formerly would
have called 'heavy'.

There was a series of lectures on general subjects given at
Changi Cinema. Harry attended a lecture on earthquakes:

7 JULY 1942

Most hopeful part is that Japan has a big quake
about once every 20 years – her time is now up.

There were also lectures on car maintenance, which Harry
thought would be useful after the war:

16 MAY 1942

I now know how to decoke a car but I doubt whether
I would practise on my own. I wondered how my
Hillman & Standard were getting on in England.
They will be very useful after the war as cars will be
very scarce.

One talk he really enjoyed was given by the Australian
wicketkeeper Ben Barnett on his Test match experiences:

22 AUGUST 1942

He spoke for quite a while about that exciting Test
match at Leeds, when they won on the 3rd day and
I knelt on the gravel all day watching them. He had
a fund of good stories to relate.

He particularly relished the lectures on current affairs and
noted in detail the topics discussed. Combined with the news
gleaned from the illegal radios, Harry had a good knowledge
of the battles in Europe and North Africa. One lecture was
given by General Percival on the BEF in France and the
reasons for its failure. He learned from another talk about the
disastrous Battle of Mersa Matruh in Egypt, which the army
barely survived:

30 JUNE 1942

It came as a shock to us – each defeat & each
evacuation increases the duration of our stay here.
It is a remarkable thing when one comes to recount
British victories on land in this war. How we always
muddle through to victory is amazing.

Harry and his friends would chat about the lectures and latest
news:

22 FEBRUARY 1942

It is very pleasant to sit out in the cool of the evening on the verandah or on the grass in front of the billet. We discuss the cause of our failures, individual deeds of bravery and otherwise; our future, and rumours which are numerous and often far-fetched. Some most remarkable rumours spread round and are believed by many of the troops eg The Russians are fighting on German soil, there has been an invasion of England, Rommel has been beaten, etc. It is impossible to trace the source of these 'authentic' rumours.

Many of their moonlight discussions after the 'nocturnal feed' were related to war:

30 MAY 1942

Padre is firstly of the impression that war is not inevitable & will soon cease to exist as men become more civilised. I argued that history always repeats itself – there will always be wars & that in some countries, civilisation is going backward. The nature of man cannot be altered & the bad side occasionally comes to the top with will to power → war.

Sometimes their choice of topic for discussion seemed to be quite random.

'Evening party', Changi, undated.
Harry, 2nd from R; Padre Cordingly, far L.

29 APRIL 1942

Argued until early hours of morning why water climbs up a capillary tube. Tried to remember my physics – problem remained unsolved.

Harry played bridge regularly and gave a series of bridge lessons to would-be players. He started a bridge competition, which attracted good numbers. Some Dutch officers who were billeted in the same building were regular opponents.

13 NOVEMBER 1942

I have played bridge several times against 2 very good Dutch players – their Smith 4NT convention baffles me & also them at times.

Bridge was played in the evenings, which had its disadvantages:

26 MARCH 1942

Played bridge on verandah as usual but extended the hours of play till 1030 PM by using my hurricane lamp. Drawback is the large number of little insects and animals that collect around the light.

Every evening would have some arranged activity. Harry said they were a cheerful little crowd with regular pleasant evening sessions. When there were blackouts, they entertained themselves playing quizzes and word games such as spelling bees and 'my auntie went to town'.

Harry's thirty-second birthday, and his first as a POW, was celebrated in style on 21 December in the Padre's room. He received a number of gifts and as lavish a supper party as his friends could manage:

22 DECEMBER 1942

I had a large cake made by the officers mess cookhouse, but unfortunately it collapsed in the morning & had to be supported with string & bumph – tastefully cut to make it appear decorative. I also produced my famous home-made brew ie Panther's Breath which, although there was a small portion per person, was very tasty & alcoholic –

not however sufficient to make us tipsy. All in all it was a good night's work & my first birthday in a POW camp. I wonder how many more there will be. None I hope!

It is understandable that the prisoners of war made the most of every opportunity for a celebration, but none more so than Christmas, a joint celebration by the British and the Dutch. On their first Christmas Eve, on the green in front of the mess, there was a grand sacred concert organised by the Dutch:

25 DECEMBER 1942

It looked like a crowded fairground from our position on the balcony. It ended up with the fire ceremony, which is a symbolic affair – the fire represents the spirit of life and freedom which keeps burning, and the Dutch 'broadcast' a message to their wives and families in front of the fire, and then each one took a burning rod and lit a candle in his own tent. The association of flame with life is a very common one in many religions. It was quite a dramatic affair, as all the lights were doused, and only the flickering fire played on the announcer's face as he spoke in a loud voice to the families at home. Our padre translated it into English for the benefit of the non-Dutch.

Harry described their first Christmas Day in captivity as 'a day of mutual compliments and bright atmosphere. There is a tremendous menu arranged which will satisfy every gourmand and gourmet.' One of the highlights of their Christmas dinner was the absence of rice! It consisted of 'chicken soup, fish creole, roast chicken, and 3 veg including new potatoes, Xmas pudding, savoury, wine (home-made)'. The cooks had obviously been planning this festive meal for some time.

At midday the British entertained the Dutch officers to coffee and cakes, and after dinner about twenty-five British officers joined the Dutch for another party:

> Mutual congratulation speeches were made by the respective OCs [officers commanding], and we stood in silence for various reasons on numerous occasions eg Dutch royal family, Dutch wives, allied casualties, etc. Harris made a very optimistic speech in which he said that by June '43 we would be victorious, and that next Xmas we would be out of here. Time will tell.
>
> Christmas inevitably turned everyone's thoughts to home. There were many sad faces today as they read the various messages issued by various commanders. They all have one thing in common, hoping that by next Xmas we will be by our own fireside.

New Year's Eve was another justification for a party. This was held in the Padre's room:

1 JANUARY 1943

We finished off the meal by a toast to the New Year, drunk with a mixture of the Jap 'brandy', Padre's communion wine and pineapple juice. The Jap stuff was almost raw spirit, and we got about ½ cupful each. It made the troops very hilarious, and at midnight they surrounded the Padre's room, and we went out and shook hands with all and sundry. There were the usual songs eg Auld Lang Syne, followed by Blaydon Races, We're Here Because We're Here, etc. Led by a bloke banging on a tin box, the men marched up and down outside till nearly 2 AM singing and carousing. The Dutch downstairs also entered into the spirit of the thing, and altogether we passed from the old into the new year in traditional style. The general opinion seems to be that this year will see the end of the war in our favour – let us hope and pray that this will be so.

9

An Incident Unparalleled in Military History

There were many atrocities committed by the Japanese during the days leading up to capitulation, but for the first six months of captivity, POW life continued fairly uneventfully. There were frequent instances of mean-spirited bullying and temporary restrictions of liberties with a few isolated incidents of torture. The guards' behaviour was unpredictable.

18 MARCH 1943

Hedley, trying to be helpful in his capacity as amateur interpreter, put his foot in it with a Jap Corporal who proceeded to give Adrian [Hedley] a hell of a bashing with his fist, feet and rifle. This went on for several minutes and a large crowd of onlookers gathered round. It is very humiliating mentally besides the physical damage and Adrian behaved splendidly and bore it all with very good grace.

However, the prisoners learned strategies they hoped would avoid upsetting the guards, and they coped with what were mainly petty punishments.

The number of POWs in Changi had also dropped substantially as large groups were regularly shipped off to forced labour in Japan and the Dutch East Indies (now Indonesia) and also to work on the Burma–Thailand Railway. It was rare there was any news of these men, although there was much speculation about their fate. Occasionally survivors from places such as Java turned up in Changi with dreadful tales to tell of vicious treatment by the Japanese, but in general life in the camp was fairly stable. This continued until what history books have recorded as the Selarang Barracks Incident.

Selarang Barracks at the time of the 'non-escape' pledge incident.
Sketch by Charles Thrale, 1942

Four prisoners had attempted an escape from Changi but had been recaptured. Japan had not ratified the Geneva Convention, which specified standards for the humanitarian treatment of prisoners of war – including appropriate punishments for escape attempts. In fact, it was generally considered that POWs had the right and a moral duty to try to escape, and those caught should be liable to disciplinary punishment only.

However, after the abortive escape, the Japanese insisted that all the Changi POWs should sign a no-escape pledge (Harry called it 'a parole') with the following wording: 'I the undersigned, hereby solemnly swear on my honour that I will not, under any circumstances, attempt to escape.' With the exception of three internees, they refused to sign, as this would contravene one of the terms of the Geneva Convention, and the whole POW camp was sent to Selarang Barracks as penalty. Although this number did not include the 2,500 sick and dying in the camp hospital, many more were unfit and had enormous difficulties on the two-mile march to Selarang.

Harry gave a full, graphic account of this and subsequent events in his long diary entry for Sunday 6 September 1942:

We have taken part in an incident unparalleled in Military History. The events in order are:

August 30th The Japs gave us the opportunity of signing a certificate stating that under no circumstances would we on our honour attempt escape. Naturally we all refused to sign as it is against

British Military Law to give parole voluntarily. Also the question of honour being involved we could not sign in case a good opportunity ever occurred. On the night of 30/31 Col. Holmes gave this verdict to the Japs.

The following day the Japs changed their former request to an order, which the C-in-C [Commander-in-Chief] refused to obey pointing out as above that we are not permitted to sign. On the night of Sept 1st/2nd, the C-in-C was sent for by the Japs and told that by 6 PM the following day we all had to move to Selarang Barracks which was to be a prison for the whole P of W Camp and 'measures of severity' would be applied to us till we signed.

Consequently the following day there was an early morning conference and a flap lasting till midday when the order came to march off about 3 PM. Not knowing whether we would come back or not, all stores as far as possible were taken, reserve rations were given out, library books and tools were scattered among the men, medical stores were loaded on the ambulance which also towed two full water tank trucks – loaded full, with kit, sick men, tables etc.

The motley procession that set off was a remarkable sight. Ovens, stoves, containers were all taken including firewood and rations on small trucks loaded to a height of 10–12 feet. Men carried their belongings slung on bamboo poles and the move was carried out in good spirit, the men being very cheerful and light-hearted. The C-in-C complimented the men on this in an Order of the Day. We didn't know what to do with our livestock so the ducks were carried upside down by officers and the chickens were left.

It is fortunate they took so much with them: their provisions helped to supplement the very meagre rations they were given. Selarang Barracks had originally been part of the British Changi Garrison built to accommodate 1,600 men. After the surrender it had been taken over by the Japanese to house the Australian internees. Now it was to hold 17,000. The Japanese restricted the area even further, deliberately excluding all the existing latrines. This meant that there was an immediate necessity to dig fresh latrines through the concrete square into which they were all crammed.

There was a march of about 2 miles to our new home in the former Australian area at Selarang. This consists of barrack blocks on 3 sides of a square with a concrete courtyard in the centre. 18th Division had 2 blocks with the threat that if the Hospital also moved, one block would be taken from us. It was estimated that three to five hundred men would die if the hospital were moved – just by the move alone. The Japs postponed this drastic step. As it was, each man had 6 x 2 ft of space – just enough for a man to lie down without moving.

Thousands slept outside on the concrete with no protection from the rain. We were fortunate as we were on a verandah on the 1st floor facing outwards and had about 1 ft of space between camp beds. Batmen slept at our feet in the narrow space left. The officers on the ground floor verandah were badly off as the malarial drains that ran past their heads were used for excretion purposes both liquid and solid. Consequently the first night the stink was terrific.

There were two water-points for the whole area water limited to one gallon per man for all purposes – queuing up for 2–3 hours was common. No washing or shaving was the order.

One small MI room was available for all the sick. I was appointed MO for Div Troops 10.30–12 each morning. But as the position was chaotic and impossible, I took all my stores to the ambulance and rigged up a little MI room there. Only the urgent and acute cases were seen. No ordinary dressings or treatments were done. The Aussies fortunately had set up a hospital tent in the middle and were doing dentistry and operations. There was an acute appendix done the first night by lamplight as the Japs said 'no communication with hospital'.

Flies were increasing in number and swill etc was accumulating. Latrines were dug all through the first night; the men worked like Trojans, digging long rows of trenches 16 ft deep while the sappers made latrine tops from doors of billets, men were sleeping on the roofs and all over the courtyard except for space for cookhouses and latrines. The road running round the billet was out of bounds and the Jap sentries beat up anyone treading on the road. A machine gun was mounted on one corner and surrounded with barbed wire.

The worst feature of the day was the shooting of the four men who tried to escape. Two Aussies, one RAOC and one Gordon Highlander (two of them were in hospital with malaria and were dragged out of bed) were taken to the seashore and kept waiting for 30 minutes in the boiling sun. A firing party consisted of 4 Sikhs. The Division Commanders and the ACG [Assistant Chaplain General] were summoned to watch. The ACG was allowed a few minutes with each man first. He said that their bearing was wonderful, stood up straight, refused bandages to the eyes and although wounded in the arms and legs by the first few shots remained standing till mortally wounded. Not a groan escaped their lips. It took about 20 minutes and 27 shots were fired – a beastly and brutal affair. The Sikhs then had to bury the dead. This demonstration was supposed to cower us.

A medical section was sent from Roberts Hospital – given an hour's notice to pack etc and arrived without food or cooking facilities – even the fatigue men who pushed the trucks were kept in. The important question was a medical one, whether we could keep on living under such circumstances. All the latrine space was bound to be used up fairly soon and men were already making a mess over most of the area. Without proper washing facilities, diseases spread by direct contact – as well as by flies – were a grave danger. There were diphtheria contacts scattered among the men and there was no antitoxin for treatment.

The first day there were about 40 cases of dysentery and 22 were allowed by the Japs to go to Roberts Hospital. There were constant conferences between our chiefs and the Japs – we were trying to get the certificate altered to show that it was an order to sign. The Japs stated that they had orders from Tokyo to get the original certificate signed at all costs and every means would be used. Rations would be cut down to a third, water by a half and the accommodation by a third until we gave in.

It became obvious that we couldn't hold out very long under those conditions and reluctantly the C-in-C agreed to sign under duress. The Sappers were united in not signing until actually ordered to do so. They may have been misled by the wonderful spirit of the men. It was an amazing sight. The courtyard looked like Hyde Park with its flickering lights, men sleeping all over the place, concerts going on in every corner, pianos playing for sing-songs, men feverishly digging latrines by lamp light.

One impromptu concert had a hilarious 'slap-team' comedian.

The officers queued up with the men for meals from the cookhouse and balancing a hot plate and a mug in one hand, tried to negotiate the steps against a surging downward tide. The Padre held a short evening service on Thursday night Sept 3rd – anniversary of the outbreak of war.

On Friday 4th we cut down our rations in case we had to stay at Selarang for some time. Fortunately the canteen stores which had been brought along lasted out – we got tinned herring, soup, vegemite and cigarettes. This helped to supplement our meagre meals. I was the only MO on duty and had a short session morning and afternoon – altogether in the 3 days there I sent 13 men to hospital.

Harry was struck by the incredible spirit of the men, in spite of all the difficulties and deprivation. Jim Bradley, in his memoir, noted the guards could not understand how they could put on a concert show and said that 'the pluck of these men in such appalling conditions was totally incomprehensible to them'.

On 4 September Lieutenant-Colonel Holmes issued a written order to the effect that the Imperial Japanese Army's original requirement that all ranks of the POW camp Changi should be given the opportunity to sign a certificate of promise not to escape had now been amended to a definite order that all officers, NCOs and men of the POW camp shall sign this undertaking:

I therefore now order that these certificates will be signed by all ranks, and handed by Area Commanders to Command Headquarters by 1100 hrs on 5 September '42. The circumstances in which I have been compelled to issue this order will be made the subject of Selarang Special Order No. 3 which will be issued later.

Many of the POWs signed using false or meaningless names. One of the most common signatures among the Australians was 'Ned Kelly'.

On Friday we all signed two copies of the Jap form. The C-in-C issued a special Order of the Day (No 3) in which he outlined the events leading up to it and the reasons why he ordered us to sign. It was obvious to any sane man that we couldn't live long under such circumstances. The medical authorities estimated that after a month there would be up to 50% dead from dysentery and the remainder would probably be too weak to carry on the essential fatigues, eg fetching water, cooking, cleaning, making latrines etc. The question of the dead was difficult as they would have to be interred in the courtyard as that was the only area available. If there were many dead and dying the place would be a shambles.

To spare the lives of his men, Col Holmes signed and on Saturday morning we were told to pack. A heavy downpour of rain made things a bit difficult.

However by 2 PM the main party left and the trucks followed and returned again for a further load. I do not envy the Aussies having to live in that billet now as it must stink like fury. A few days hard work will be necessary to clean it up. It was estimated that 400 tons of soil and cement were dug up by the men during the two days of hard work – very good show.

We had a good view of Changi Gaol where the civilians are interned and from our bed we could see the lights go on and off every night. We wondered what the poor civilians were doing and whether they were getting similar treatment or not.

The fusiliers were the first back and what struck me forcibly was the quietness and stillness everywhere, where formerly was noise and chatter. There was very little missing from our billets and what was missing must have been taken by our rear party. We soon settled down to normal, brushed out the dust, unpacked and had a shower and a clean change of clothing and everything was again ante bello. The organ and prayer desk were safely brought back by the Padre and his willing band of helpers. The only ones to be put out by our return were the birds who appeared to have inhabited our billet during our absence. However we are now back safe and sound and it is a closed chapter.

As the parole had been signed under duress, it was not valid in Allied eyes, but the POWs were allowed to return to Changi. The Japanese general Fukuei Shimpei, who had ordered the unlawful, inhumane killing of the escapees, was himself executed for war crimes on exactly the same spot in April 1946. The Selarang Barracks Incident is said to be the closest concentration of human beings since the Black Hole of Calcutta.

10

Interlude

Weeks passed in Changi very much as before. A few days after returning from Selarang there is Harry's first mention of the Burma Railway.

15 SEPTEMBER 1942

There was news of the mainland party – Webb's crowd who are said to be 50 miles from Bangkok and are building a railway into Burma and constructing huts for 15,000 men. The latter has given rise to much speculation and it is generally feared that it will be meant for us.

While existing prisoners in Changi were being sent up country, large numbers of other captives arrived.

19 SEPTEMBER 1942

Yesterday about 1,000 men and officers, mostly RAF but some Army and Navy arrived here from Java. They were dirty and thin with closely cropped hair. They had been cooped up in the hold of a ship for four days. They had a bitter tale to tell. They have not been treated as well as us and have been constantly under Jap supervision. Beatings up were frequent and four officers were shot after being beaten up each day for a week. October 10th: Americans have arrived from Java and also some chaps from Kuala Lumpur who are in a bad state physically and hygienically.

23 OCTOBER 1942

Rumours of a move received official confirmation today. Large parties are moving off up country starting from the 29th. 4,500 are going from this Division.

These numbers were supplemented by captives from other areas:

Hundreds of Javanese are arriving in the camp on their way up north. They are all shades of colour from white Dutch to black natives. They have no colour question, everyone being equal. This solves a lot of difficulties and one which the British are finding very hard to solve with their coloured and Eurasian bar.

1 NOVEMBER 1942

Large parties are going away daily and the area is becoming gradually denuded.

9 JANUARY 1943

Several hundred Aussies have arrived here from Timor via Java.

Thousands more Dutch arrived in Changi over a number of days, replacing the British who were leaving.

The Japanese enjoyed filming the reluctant prisoners for propaganda purposes:

14 FEBRUARY 1943

The past few days have been completely beggared up by a desire of our captors to film us en masse. Consequently we were awakened at 6 AM – pitch black – pouring with rain – early breakfast – stand out on parade at 8 AM and were just about to start off when it was cancelled. The following day the same procedure occurred but we got out to the Padang about 1 mile away where 15,000 troops were drawn up in files. After waiting in the wet for 2 hours, the filming was postponed owing to bad light. The following morning the parade was cancelled before we started off, but took place in the afternoon – when I was fortunate enough to be excused. The other fellows were out for 5 hours, most of which was spent ankle-deep in pools of mud and the Japs are believed to have taken a quick film of their backs – so much for the week's excitement and activity.

Harry had a strong sense of the absurd:

3 JULY 1942

The Japs have the habit of arresting the orderly officer who is going out in the evening to inspect the British guard that is mounted to prevent us escaping! Sounds like Gilbert & Sullivan.

They all enjoyed stories that showed the prisoners getting the better of the Japanese:

31 DECEMBER 1942

In Singapore, Australian soldiers in charge of a steam roller for mending roads used to call at Jap HQ every day to collect 4 gallons of petrol. This went on for 4 months before the Japs realised that a steam roller doesn't need petrol. Meanwhile the petrol was sold to the Chinese at a good profit.

Sunday 14 February 1943 marked the anniversary of the fall of Singapore:

> It is now a year since we capitulated that fateful Sunday when the 'impregnable fortress', 'the bastion', 'bristling with guns' etc gave in to the Japs. Padre held a memorial service for the long list of RNF men who had fallen in battle. A year seems so long when one looks ahead, but this year has passed quickly and judged by the prevailing POW standards, very comfortably.

This was soon to change.

11

Hell in the Jungle

For many years companies from different countries had tried to build a railway from Singapore through Malaya, Thailand and Burma into India. All the plans had failed because of the difficult terrain of dense jungle and high mountains. With the Japanese success in war, there were thousands of POWs who were an excellent source of unpaid labour – again contrary to the Geneva Convention, which forbids using POWs as forced labour.

Japan needed the railway to bring soldiers and supplies up to the Burma–India border. They estimated that the project would take fifteen months. In fact, by employing their captured POWs, it took just twelve months – and thousands of deaths. It needed a huge workforce, and the Japanese accomplished this by sending overlapping labour parties of prisoners further and further north.

The Japanese had started sending regular parties of POWs up country from June 1942. No news about what happened there had filtered back to Changi, and the Japanese encouraged the belief that conditions there were better than in Singapore. In fact, the previous October, Harry had actually sent up country most of the painful-feet cases and other cases of vitamin deficiency 'in the hope that the change of air and food may cure them, for frankly there is no cure here'. They had heard that most of the travel was by truck or train, and although there was a two-day march at the end, the sick and lame would be allowed to travel by truck.

By April 1943 there were fewer than ten thousand prisoners left in Changi. Harry was assigned to F Force, a party of seven thousand British and Australian troops. It was the last group to go, and 30 per cent of this party were classed as unfit either to march or work. Jim Bradley said that most of the relatively fit men also had some kind of medical history since capitulation, and nearly all of them were reduced in strength owing to malnutrition.

HQ issued an order detailing the reasons why the move up country would be beneficial. It is unsurprising that everyone wanted to be included.

* The food situation in Singapore was difficult. A good canteen would be available in each camp and would be far better in the new place.
* This would not be a working party.
* They were going to a cooler climate in a pleasant hill place.
* The unfit men would have a better chance of recovery and good facilities for recreation.

*   There would be no marching except for a short distance from the train to a nearby camp, and transport would be provided for baggage and men unfit to march.

The group was encouraged to take band instruments, lighting sets, tools and their cooking gear. They were told that gramophones, blankets, clothing and mosquito nets would be issued at the new camps. The force would include a medical party of about 350, with equipment for a central hospital of 400 patients and medical supplies for three months.

Everyone was in a party mood, and the Japanese seemed especially lenient during the preparations for the journey. There is a jovial tone to the diary entry for 10 April 1943:

> We are nearing the end of our stay in Changi. A party of 7,000, half British and half Australian, is going up country 'to a cooler climate' in a week or so's time. It is believed that North Malaya is a probable destination. When divisional HQ decided to go, everyone thought that this was a good thing, and much intrigue is going on to be included in the party.

At first neither Harry nor the Padre were included. They relied on string-pulling and the influence of senior officers so that they too could benefit(!) from this new camp.

Harry and his team prepared carefully for the move:

18 APRIL 1943

Windmill, my medical orderly, has been working like a Trojan. He cleaned out a wooden medical box which he painted and stencilled with my name, and I have now converted it to my own use. He also made me a small, white, first aid box with all the necessary contents included. My haversack or pack he converted into a rucksack that clips on in front, and is adjustable. Two ammunition pouches that are stitched to the sides are very useful for holding toilet articles, etc.

Harry kept his basic medical kit canvas roll with him throughout. Apart from bandages and dressings, it is still intact and preserved with his other war memorabilia.

There is now a gap of over four weeks in Harry's diaries. His next, very long, entry on 23 May 1943 – with a complete change of tone – was titled *HELL IN THE JUNGLE*:

I am now seated in my own small portion of a leaky atap hut, during a storm in an unknown camp near the Burma border in northern Thailand. The journey from Changi to here almost defies description. It is a tale of hardship, suffering, hunger, thirst and disease, in conditions which could never have previously been imposed in a civilised society and which have taken their toll on the health of the men. Truth is stranger than fiction, and we have come up against conditions which would seem unbelievable in a novel.

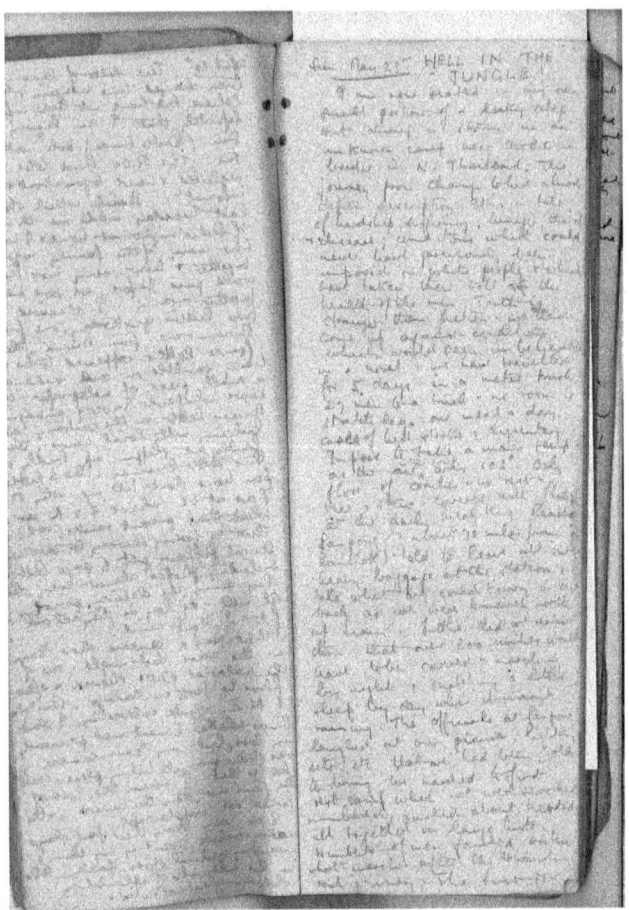

Diary, 23 May 1943, northern Thailand: 'Hell in the Jungle'

The party left Singapore by train and travelled in metal rice trucks, which were totally enclosed and unventilated apart from sliding doors in the centre of one side. Inside, the men were packed like sardines. There was no sanitation. Many of the POWs had dysentery and, in order to relieve themselves, had to hang out of the doors held by a chain.

> We left Singapore and travelled for five days in a metal truck, 27 men to a truck. No room to stretch one's legs, and one meal a day. There were numerous cases of heatstroke and dysentery. It was impossible to take a man's temperature as the air in the trucks was about 103°. The floors of the trucks were filthy and oily. There was no way we could rest. Rice and stew covered with flies formed the main meal of the day.

Acute thirst was a major problem. They stopped once a day for the fly-covered rice meal. This journey lasted for five days, the last twenty-four hours without food or water, ending at Ban Pong railway station.

The Japanese officials said they had to leave everything including precious medical equipment, taking only what they could carry in their backpacks for the long trek to northern Thailand. Vital medical supplies were distributed to those fit enough to carry them, but their backpacks were already very heavy. The short march to the first camp after the gruelling train journey was too much for the many unfit men who were just out of hospital in Changi. The realisation of the truth about 'good rest camps' was starting to hit home:

> We reached Bampong, our first stop, which I think is about 70 miles from Bangkok, and we were told to leave all our heavy baggage at the station, and

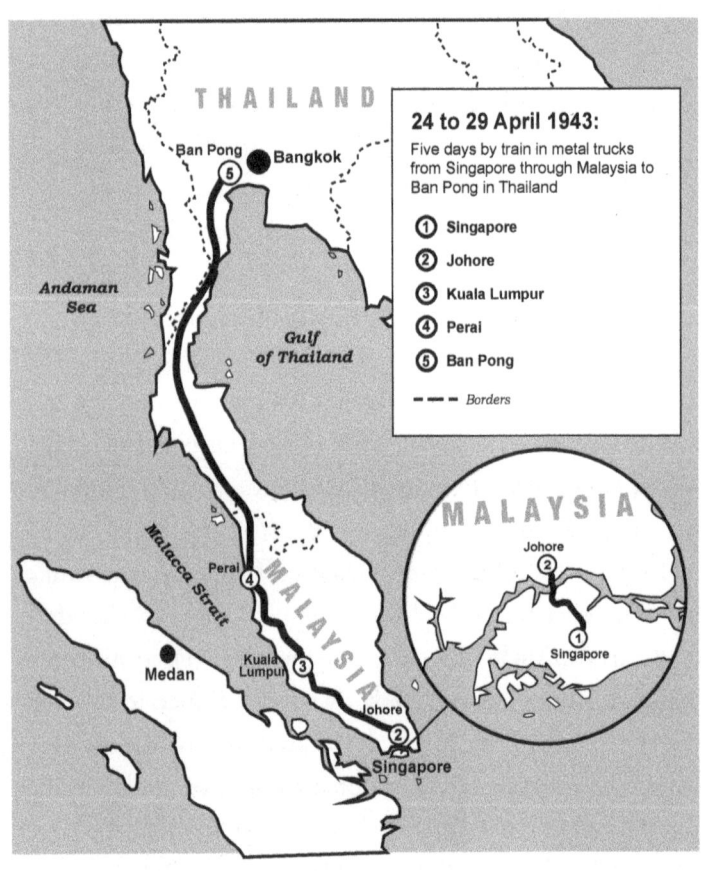

Five days by train: Singapore to Ban Pong,
24–29 April 1943

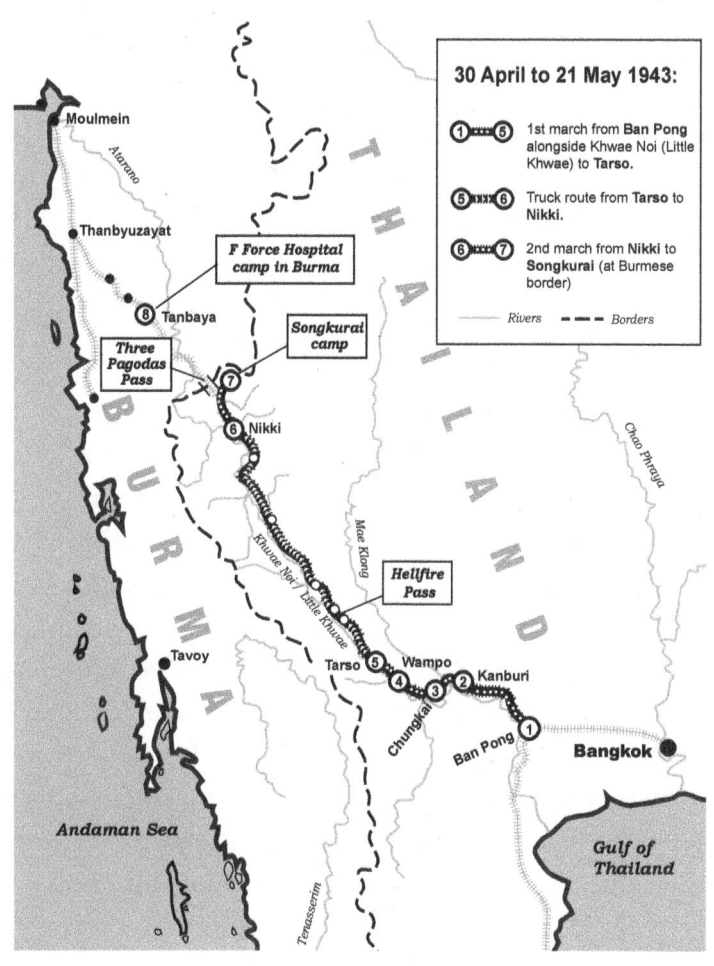

Route up country alongside the Burma Railway,
30 April–21 May 1943

take what we could carry on our back, as we were to march to Thailand. Little did we realise then that over 200 miles would have to be covered, marching by night and snatching a little sleep by day when it wasn't raining. The officials at Bampong laughed at our pianos, lighting sets, etc. that we had been told to bring.

We marched to the first rest camp where we were searched, numbered, pushed about, and herded altogether in large huts. Numbers of men fainted on the short march after the exhausting rail journey. The first MI room that we came to had about 200 patients, which each succeeding medical officer took over for one day before he started off himself again marching.

They had one night's rest, but it was impossible to sleep, before beginning their 200-mile march. This would have been a problem for fit men in reasonable territory, but it was horrendous in dense mountainous jungle and the monsoon climate. They marched by night as it was too hot during the day, carrying everything on their backs, eventually discarding the heavier items as help was needed to carry the sick. They toiled through pitch-black night and torrential rainstorms. It wasn't surprising that men fell off the mountainsides and bridges in the dark, and there were many fractured arms and legs from falls. Stragglers were attacked by Thai marauders.

Each night march covered about 15 to 20 miles. This may not sound much, but when only two-thirds of the men are fit when leaving Changi, exhausted by a long, stifling train journey, having to carry all their kit on their backs, struggling through jungle paths and swamps, and often through tropical storms on very poor rations, with diarrhoea rife, struggling on night after night, with blistered feet, very few medical supplies – all these throw a different light on the picture. At the rest camps, there were no tents. One just had to find shade under a tree. If it rained, one waited, shivering, for it to stop, and then build a fire to dry out one's clothing.

Some rest camps provided good food, and one could buy from the natives things like coffee, eggs, bananas, etc. These kept the men going. They raised money by selling their kit to the natives who paid good prices for KD [khaki drill]. I sold a few surplus items but stuck to my blankets, sheets and mosquito net which I later had to throw away, with my little hand bag which had been my constant companion since the beginning of the war. This annoyed me very much later because I could have sold the stuff I threw away, probably getting about $30–40 for it. Instead of which, I had no blankets and no money, so was not able to purchase much food.

I was medical officer in charge of my train party and marched at the tail end of the column which often straggled out for several hundred yards.

Consequently, at a halt, I treated the stragglers and by the time I caught up with the main group, the halt was almost over. I had really the world's worst job of assisting the sick, lame and the weary, supporting them, carrying stretchers, and helping with their kit, in spite of my own kit which I had to carry.

Jim Bradley wrote about the work of doctors on the march:

First [the doctors] would be called to a casualty falling back at the rear of the column, and next they would be wanted up front. When we arrived at our staging camps, completely without shelter, we would throw ourselves on the ground and perhaps take off our boots if we dared … The doctors, however, held sick parades, attending to men's blistered and burnt feet, and doing what they could for the sick and dying. They took little time to rest themselves, but I believe they received scant recognition for all they did, except in the gratitude which showed on the faces of all those whom they helped.

Harry's diary entry continues:

The fifth night march took its toll of my health. I had been losing weight, had diarrhoea, and tenosynovitis of my tendoachilles. My mental and physical condition can be imagined as I struggled on through a tropical storm, through water, swirling and rushing waist-high on two occasions. One of my shoes was torn off, so I discarded the other one and completed the journey barefooted. Every step was agony. I had never realised before what it meant to go through such a night of mental and physical torture.

Meagre rations consisted of rice and water. Most rest camps had no tents, just clearings in the jungle. They tried to find shade from the sun or shelter from the rain under trees. Many hundreds died on the way up country, mostly from malnutrition, malaria and dysentery. At one rest camp Harry himself was classed as unfit to march further by a Japanese MO.

The rest camp reached the following morning, Tarso, was a big Jap headquarters and contained a lot of British, including several of the former up country parties. Major Harris and Major Wild were waiting at the camp to receive us. I must have looked pretty bad as Harris and GI each came fussing round, bringing me tea, etc. Hutch and Dillon treated me very well when I lived with them in their tent for the following five days. I was left behind to act as the medical officer in charge of the MI room in Tarso, partly because of my poor physical condition and partly because there was need for one there.

I saw the Jap MO who passed me unfit to march. He was very strict and examined all the men who were left behind who were marked unfit to travel.

He sent on cases of diarrhoea, dysentery, septic and blistered feet, etc. It made my blood boil to see the weary men with large, swollen and septic feet, infected blisters and ulcers, having to hobble away at night. I can feel for them, as I know what they went through.

After five days, Harry was allowed to continue the next stage of the journey by truck, accompanying the sick:

Hutch very kindly arranged for me to continue the journey by truck so I could arrive at the final destination fairly fresh, and receive the incoming parties. Little did I realise that each stage of the journey was worse than its predecessor.

Travelling by truck sounds good, but going on a heavy five tonner through a Thai jungle, up and down very steep slopes, across dangerous swaying bamboo bridges which broke under the wheels, clinging on to the baggage on which we were so precariously balanced, bumping incessantly up and down till all parts of our bodies were sore, seeing the back wheels skid on the slippery edge of a precipice as we looked down from the truck straight onto the water fifty or sixty feet below and going across the sides of a quarry on a rough road made out of shifting stone, pushing the truck several miles when it broke down, climbing off and on to push it out of muddy ruts, keeping back the shifting machinery, red-hot from the sun, blistering our backs and hands, seeing two trucks overturn going over narrow bridges and dropping into the valley below – that's what driving by truck meant. I went forward in the truck to take the injured men from the first overturned truck to the base hospital which was fifteen miles away when our truck broke down with a broken differential.

We were stranded for twenty-four hours by the roadside with a query fractured skull and numerous cases of minor injuries plus one query intestinal injury. Finally we were marched two miles back to the last camp. The Australians were there with a small MI room. Major Stevens and Major Hunt, Australian MOs, were there and I lived with them in their tent for two days. I was very comfortable there.

Harry continued the journey on foot, but

then my troubles started again. Some Burmese coolies, who were doing roofing, lived amongst the Australian troops, and they were dying like flies in and around the cookhouse and were fouling the ground. It was only after a couple of days had elapsed that it was discovered that cholera was the cause of death of these coolies. By that time, it was too late, as cholera had clearly spread to the troops, some of whom had only had one injection before leaving Changi.

The ground was covered with infected faeces, but the Japanese refused to lend spades to the British officers who wanted to remove this dreadful health hazard, and said 'use your hands'.

> Inoculation was feverishly given, and all the troops were moved out to another camp. I moved a few hundred yards down the road with the sick to isolate them, and was parked in the jungle with numerous sandflies and mosquitoes. Parties came and went and it was only after three days, alone in the jungle, with no covering or medical supplies, that a truck was provided to take me and my little party forward.

F Force had to trudge past many work camps, when they learned there was cholera in the camp. G. P. Adams, in his book *No Time for Geishas*, said that people in these camps would watch F Force plodding past: 'However sorry we may have been for ourselves, our hearts could bleed for the unfortunates of F Force who passed by our camp for days on end. All were tired and worn.'

Harry continues:

> We reached base headquarters where we found the other British train parties settled in. A hospital had been established, but the huts had no roofs. A very small stream provided water for all the camp, and conditions generally were not good. The only good feature was the Jap commanding officer who

worked hard on our behalf. We stayed in the camp for two days, and I was just about settling in when I was ordered to move on with train 7 to their final destination, 15 kilometres further along the road.

Once again I set off on a night march, leaving at 1 AM, and getting to the new camp the following morning. We passed the Australian camp after 10km where they were having trouble with numerous cases of cholera and were short of medical officers. We were certainly glad to reach our final destination after so many so-called 'final' ones. And so ended the long and weary trek through 200 miles of wild jungle to our new home where we may stay till the end of the war. The condition of the men as they arrived beggars description – no boots, tattered clothes, sunken cheeks, unshaven faces. It was often impossible to recognise old friends. However the relief of being able to lie down and sleep at night surpasses all else.

Harry had tried in this diary entry to record events chronologically as he remembered them, but he continued to add more specifics:

I will now try to fill in a few details as they occur to me. They are bound to be disjointed, but will bring back certain interesting events to the memory. One of the most amusing was the sight of men completing their march by hailing cycle carriages, and finishing the journey in style. Some even stopped to buy fruit from vendors by the roadside while the guards waited.

This particular camp sold fried eggs, meat, etc, and the men tucked in with gusto. Selling kit – one's own, and some that I suspect was stolen – went with a swing all along the line of communications. The natives paid good money, especially for shirts and shorts. I sold one or two things, and managed to scrape up five dollars.

Harry said frequently that captivity brought out the best and worst in men:

On one or two occasions, Major Barber who was OC managed to stop a truck for the lame and sick. There was a disgusting scramble for lifts by fit men. At times like this, I was very disappointed by the behaviour of some of the men who were very selfish. By the end of the journey, in spite of the difficulties, I ceased to have much sympathy for them.

He would grab a few minutes' respite whenever he could:

I used to have difficulty sleeping on the hard ground or strange bed. The few minutes rest we had at each halt would see me throw myself down where I stood, on the muddy road, and fall fast asleep till awakened all too soon, stiff and weary, to continue the agony. I made the mistake originally of trying to take too much kit, and suffered from the heavy pack on my back. It felt much lighter when the blanket and mosquito net were discarded.

The MI rooms in the rest camps were hastily improvised shelters, and often had no covering at all. The MOs left behind to look after the sick had a difficult job with no supplies and very few facilities for treatment. In most of the camps I did my own sick parade, often very large, while the rest of the men and officers were sleeping. The job of a medical officer was very arduous, and I often went for days without a proper rest.

Looking back on our journey, the five days in the train when we left Changi which then were thought to be the height of discomfort, were at times almost unbelievable. The heat from the metal roof was burning to the fingers. The absence of a cooling draught of air made us look like dirty rags after a few days.

The one meal a day left us terribly hungry and thirsty. Fortunately the Nip guards allowed us to descend at most of the stations and buy food. The hot sweet coffee and hard-boiled eggs that I bought at dawn at Alastare will always be in my memory as one of the most welcome meals I have ever had. We stuffed ourselves with papaya, bananas and eggs at each halt, so we managed to keep going. We were able to wash when we stopped by a river. At one place we had to do PT [physical training]!

Major Wild had a very difficult job and succeeded very well. Evidence of partial destruction of bridges, etc by the British during the retreat was still visible, but repair work had been efficiently carried out. The causeway which was supposed to have been blown up was as good as new. The Chinese were quite friendly, but were obviously afraid of the Japs.

The final journey by truck was the most exciting, and for my green medical case to come through unscathed after being hurled twice into the ravine was a miracle. I had a two-volt battery lamp, a dinner plate and a mirror, all unbroken, and good testimony to the packer. Elephants are very useful, pushing heavy tree trunks out of impossible positions, and can do the work of fifty men.

The most annoying part of the journey was the way four or five Nips would all shout out different orders together whenever the truck got into difficulties. They are very excitable and flare up quickly. If any part, eg a petrol pump, is being repaired, one of them watches the British driver doing the job and then takes the bit himself and repeats it, often very badly.

It upset Harry greatly that the weakened men were expected to clear the tracks for the troops:

It pained me to see the thin bodies of men heaving stones from the side of the quarry and they are expected to keep going on poor rations. How they can do this hard work is beyond my comprehension.

For two nights we shared tents with Nips. They are very neat and tidy but take most of the room, and we were closely crowded. On the whole, the guards who accompanied us treated us fairly well. It was the Nips at the halts who beat the men and made officers do general fatigues and cookhouse duties. Beatings were all too common. I am looking forward to the day when it will all be repaid with interest.

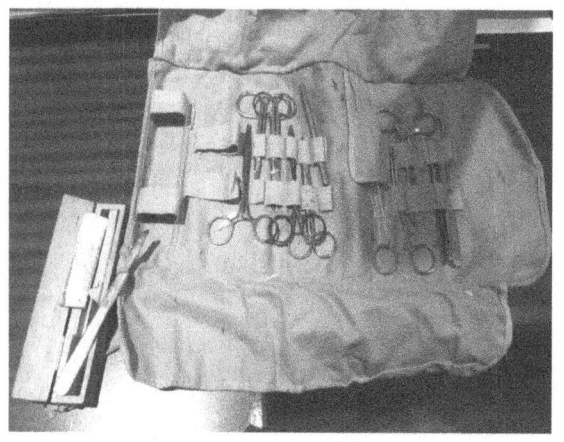

Harry's green medical kit

12

You Couldn't Eat a Cigarette Case

They had reached Songkurai in Thailand, near the Three Pagodas Pass, and Harry stayed in this area for ten weeks.

27 MAY 1943

We arrived here six days ago, very weary and tired, with large numbers of sick. Two large unroofed huts were given to the men and a smaller atap hut was allotted to the officers. At the far end, the Japanese soldiers are sleeping. Unfortunately for the first 48 hours it poured incessantly. It was the start of the monsoon season. Parties kept arriving and I was kept busy from dawn till dusk.

It was a sea of mud at the height of the monsoon, which continued for five months. It is difficult to imagine how the captives coped in uncovered huts. They slept on platforms made of split bamboo with a space of two feet wide for each man. They had no running water, no soap, no toothpaste or toilet paper. They sold whatever surplus clothes and possessions they had to local people to get money to buy food. Many of the men were reduced to wearing just loincloths.

When interviewed for *Back to the Front*, Harry said he sold a gold filling from his teeth plus precious items he had managed to save up to this point: his gold watch, (which had been a graduation present from his father), his wallet and a cigarette case: 'You couldn't eat a cigarette case very well. My thoughts were only for survival.'

On one occasion Harry was the only 'fit' person, and he collected the wherewithal to buy eggs. He bought about six dozen, a supply which he intended to eke out over a number of days for his sick patients. Walking back to the camp his heart sank when a Japanese guard on a passing railway truck forced him at bayonet point onto the train. As he neared the camp and was able to see smoke from the fires, the guard, with an evil grin, caused the train to pick up speed. Harry had no option but to jump backwards from the truck, trying in vain to protect his precious bundle of eggs. That night POWs in the hospital benefited from an enormous omelette made with the eggs, including the broken shells and bits of fluff from inside his pack.

The captives were grateful to the brave men who, at risk of being shot if discovered, had carried radio parts in their packs during the long trek through the jungle. Using the battery the Japanese guards allowed Harry to have for lighting the MI room, the prisoners were able to keep up to date with news of the war in Europe. The radio components were hidden in the hollow bamboo chair legs and the waste pipes of the sink in Harry's MI room. However, this involved great risk, punishable by death, and every so often he cut out tiny sections of the diaries that would have indicated to the Japanese that he had access to an illegal radio. (These holes did not help when transcribing the diaries!)

The construction of the Burma Railway was a huge project made much harder by the fact that the Japanese provided no heavy construction equipment. The prisoners built the railway entirely by hand. They broke the ground with pickaxes and shovels. They moved earth with buckets and bamboo-and-burlap litters. Stone crushing for ballast was done with hammers. To bore holes in hard rock they used iron drills and sledgehammers.

The men had to work under exceptionally terrible conditions, being treated like slaves with daily beatings using wire whips and sticks of bamboo. One punishment was to be made to stand holding a heavy rock above one's head for hours in the full sun with a sharpened bamboo stick propped against the prisoner's back. If he wavered, as inevitably happened, the bamboo stick pierced his skin. If he dropped the rock at any point without permission, he was beaten. Some guards just threw rocks at the prisoners for fun. When the guards finally accepted that a prisoner was too ill to work on the railway, they would stop his rations as he was now of no use to them. These men were kept alive solely on rice shared by 'active' men from their own rations.

Along the Burma Railway, Thailand, c. 1942–43

At one point Harry was sent to Force HQ as a special messenger, where he met up with the Australian MOs:

27 MAY 1943

We walked most of the way there except for two miles when we tried to get a lift on a passing truck, but as we spent ages pulling the truck out of swamps, pools, ditches, etc, we decided it was quicker to walk. The Aussie working parties are working till late in the evening and coming back well soaked. They have to eat in the darkness and try and dry their clothes before they get to bed. Major Hunt with the two MOs has got his hands full in the Aussie camp. They had 40 cases of cholera up to two days ago, and this has been increasing daily.

It was to be expected that the food situation would be worse here than in Changi. Although rice was plentiful, there were virtually no vitamins or minerals in their food. When they could, they made use of local livestock for protein:

27 MAY 1943

We have a collection of rather emaciated yaks, two of which are killed off each day, and we have a tasty stew at night. Otherwise the meals are rice and a thin stew of onions or beans. A large number of men, especially officers, have gross oedema of the legs, due mostly to deficient diet.

6 JUNE 1943

Yesterday some Manchester men got half a yak and a cow by doubtful means. We got a mouth-watering meal that night.

22 JUNE 1943

A large snake, five feet long was killed in the officers' quarters yesterday, and was cleaned and boiled.

Those brave enough to eat it said it tasted like chicken!

Because of the lack of hygiene, minimal food rations and slave-labour conditions the POWs suffered and died from a huge number of tropical diseases:

27 MAY 1943

Sanitary conditions are very bad, and there was no accommodation for the MI room or the hospital. The ration Jap became a patient of mine, and he let me use the ration hut as an MI room. This was a godsend. He has been very good otherwise and gave me a large quantity of sugar etc when I asked him for it, as Wilkie is a sick man and has a bad attack of dengue.

Harry sometimes worked a twenty-four-hour day, with very little in the way of medical treatment. Cholera was a major problem. It had been brought to the camps by Burmese labourers who were conscripted by the Japanese:

27 MAY 1943

This cursed cholera is the cause of the trouble. It has followed us all the way since the camp where the Burmese were dying from cholera in our cookhouse. It has spread to the Aussies who had only had one inoculation. They were moved out to another camp, but the curse has followed us.

Every day he logged the number of cholera cases and subsequent deaths. His diary entries during this time are filled with descriptions of this nightmare period:

27 MAY 1943

So far we have had about 30 cases and twelve deaths. The number of cases is increasing daily, and we are holding conferences, etc. A hygiene officer has been appointed, and everything possible is being done. At first the isolation place was an unroofed small hut in which patients lay soaking and froze to death. Now we have a roofed isolation place and the two far ends of the big hut are used for hospital accommodation. Most of the MOs are sick themselves, with either swollen feet or fever, and it is a hell of a job to keep going.

28 MAY 1943

The number of deaths from cholera is increasing, now 23, and is spreading to other units. The isolation centre is working more efficiently now. Sanitary conditions are very primitive, and the task of looking after the patients is unenviable.

30 MAY 1943

The position is going from bad to worse. There are over 100 cholera patients and there have been nearly 40 deaths. There are 18 bodies waiting to be buried today. Labour shortage for essential tasks in hospital is acute. We have no men to clean up the place or carry the food and fluids to the patients. Some cholera patients have waited 20 hours without a drink to be admitted. I have found that looking after the MI room and the hospital is really far too much for one MO, and so I am concentrating on the hospital. I appointed a messing officer for the hospital to keep up the supply of fluids to the patients. It is tragic to see all the dehydrated patients lying for hours without a drink. The one bucket that the hospital possessed has been stolen.

2 JUNE 1943

The death roll continues to mount. Yesterday the number was 62 dead and about 110 cases in hospital. The isolation place is grossly overcrowded, and the Nips say that they will build an extension later on. Meals are very poor, and I am still in a poor state. I have never been so weary in all my life. I just drag one foot after the other, leaning on a stick.

3 JUNE 1943

I have been over to the cholera centre. It looks like a scene from a film, completely unreal. There is a long, dark, atap hut, with over a hundred thin skeleton-like beings, writhing on the long platform, vomiting and passing motions where they lie. Groans and cries are the only noises to break the silence. Two or three orderlies with masks over their mouths were giving intravenous injections of saline, using Heath Robinson contraptions. About nine corpses lay outside covered with blankets and groundsheets, and a little distance away, the smoke of the pyre where the corpses are burning could be seen. We have a gruesome job here, burning the dead cholera patients. It is a terrible, tragic end to die of disease in a jungle camp like this.

For a while Harry was caring single-handedly for up to four hundred cholera patients, and he estimated that one man in ten died of cholera in the camp. It is clear from Harry's testament in *Back to the Front*, made nearly sixty years later, that these scenes were still vividly remembered:

Doing a ward round in a cholera ward, it is really indescribable. They're just writhing in agony, they've got diarrhoea, their faces are shrunken and they're just skin and bones. It was such a painful end for them. They wanted something to help them, but I had nothing to give them.

The only relief that could be provided was rehydration:

> They had to have fluids, so we would boil and cool
> water and, using my stethoscope tube and a needle
> made out of a bamboo shoot, we used to try and
> supply them with the fluids. That's what they needed.
> They needed rehydrating, but unfortunately most of
> the cholera patients died.

On 6 June, the Japanese intervened and tested all the POWs:

> Sweeping changes have taken place overnight. The
> Japs have bumstuck everyone, and a hundred and
> seventy-four men are off with 'possible' results, and
> have been sent off to the far side of the camp into
> isolation. The weather was atrocious and it poured
> down all afternoon so the move was postponed.
> The Japs got annoyed and ordered it to take place
> forthwith. So it took place in pitch darkness until the
> early hours of the morning in a terrific downpour.
> The helpless patients were floundering about in the
> mud. Some of those who fell down, stayed down,
> until they were found in the mud by other people.
> A further order that all diarrhoea patients had
> to be segregated was carried out at first light this
> morning, and the hospital was split up into two
> parts – a fever department in the lower hut, and
> a diarrhoea department in the upper one, but
> all diarrhoea men have to be segregated. Special

latrines, buckets of antiseptic, bags of lime etc have been provided, and a Jap officer from Moulmein is coming today to inspect the camp. Theoretically, the move is very sound, one I would recommend.

Another condition that affected many of the prisoners was a tropical ulcer of the legs caused by infected scratches from cut bamboo, and it spread rapidly. With the right treatment this is not a fatal disease, but the doctors had nothing that would help:

22 SEPTEMBER 1943

I saw my former batman, Windmill, today. He is in the ulcer ward, and looks a wreck of his former vigorous self. He pleaded with me with tears in his eyes for his leg to be taken off, but as he is such a bad operative risk, I understand it will not be done. He says the pain is terrific, twenty-four hours a day, and at night he is afraid of losing his reason. What a terrible thing a tropical ulcer is. Amputation is the only treatment and relief, and the post-operative mortality is very high.

Windmill did have his amputation but died a few days later – 'What a tragic end for a healthy young lad.'

It really distressed Harry that there was so little he could do for the sick. His diary records the number of deaths from disease and malnutrition each day at the railway work camps.

Every day brought fresh cases of other diseases, including malaria, dysentery, beriberi, various fevers and even smallpox and typhus. He had a number of diphtheria cases which he found very upsetting:

4 JUNE 1943

One feels so helpless. With these cases there are no antitoxins, just rest, and the men are choking to a slow and painful death.

It was predictable that many of the MOs would become ill themselves, and on one occasion Harry did a ward round carried on a stretcher after he had fainted. In September he had a type of malaria that also had symptoms of tropical typhus. The only treatment available was quinine, but it seemed to help. It lasted over a week, but he still continued his work despite feeling 'bloody awful – no appetite, nausea, dizziness, cold sweats, deafness and tinnitus'.

Jim Bradley greatly admired the way the doctors worked under such appalling conditions:

The one I remember with particular affection was Dr Harry Silman who worked ceaselessly for the benefit of all. I had known him so well in Changi, as he was one of those with whom I had sat and talked on the roof of our barrack block at night. He was always cheerful, despite our circumstances.

The Japanese guards demanded a minimum number of men to work on the railway each day. It became more and more difficult to find this number as the death toll increased daily but the guards were relentless, driving out everyone they thought could put in even the smallest amount of work.

30 MAY 1943

HQ had a conference with the Nips this morning and tried to get a moratorium on the working parties building the railway until the illness peak has passed. I am afraid that HQ will get very little sympathy from the Japs as they are blinded by the God of Road and Railway. They will find out their mistake very soon when the number of fit men is decreasing daily to almost none at all.

The doctors had the terrible task of deciding which of the sick men were least sick. In *Back to the Front*, Harry said:

In the morning, a certain number, say 60, had to go out on the working party. If I couldn't find 60 fit people, I used to tell them. It didn't make any difference. They would go along saying 'You, you, you and you, you and you'. I'd say they can't go, they're too ill. The bayonets would come out, and I knew what would happen. They'd be carried back dead.

As the Japanese had huge numbers of prisoners, the death toll was immaterial to them.

Inevitably, friends and colleagues of Harry died during this time. Each death was a tragedy:

3 JUNE 1943

We heard yesterday that John Excell died. It was a terrible shock. He was the life and soul of any mess. He had started designing my house which he called Bedside Manor!

23 JULY 1943

Sgt Armstrong, my medical sergeant from the beginning, died a few days ago from dysentery. He had put up a hard fight. I was very sad, and I was with him when he died peacefully.

The cause of death was not always illness or disease. Some could not cope with the sheer effort of staying alive. In the YTV documentary, Harry related what had happened to a warrant officer:

He was six feet three inches. A fine fellow. He really had nothing wrong with him, except that he didn't want to keep on living. When he took to his bed I used to sit and chat to him. I took his wallet out and showed him the photo of his wife and children. I said, 'Now surely you want to go back.' It was the most amazing thing. He just faded away and died.

Quite remarkably, considering the debilitated health of the captives, an escape attempt was made.

6 JULY 1943

Yesterday, a bombshell! When we got up we found that Col. Wilkinson, Robbie, Jack Feathers, Bill Anker, Jim Bradley and three other officers had slipped off during the night, and made a daring bid to escape. The Japs were very annoyed and created a hell of a flap. We were on a roll call parade for two hours and all closely questioned. Col. Banyo imposed a penalty of five days starvation on all the officers, and said that next time, Col. Hingston would be shot. Fortunately the ban on food was lifted for MOs and officers on working parties. Food was secretly slipped in to the others during the night. I thought how marvellous it must be to reach safety and freedom, but I don't think that the risk is worth it.

12 JULY 1943

Because of the escape, the present relatively friendly Nips are being replaced by a group of 30 unfriendly Nips and an officer. They patrol day and night. We have now been warned that if anyone else tries to escape, we will ALL be shot.

Four of the eight escapees, including Jim Bradley, were caught and were extremely fortunate to be imprisoned and not executed.

Harry was relocated from one camp to another, according to where his medical services were needed. In one camp food rations were very poor, and he was part of a ration party sent to collect food from another eight miles away.

15 JUNE 1943

On my journey to the camp to pick up supplies, the truck stalled, and with the brakes not working, we ran backwards downhill at a fast pace and ended up in a stream at a very acute angle. We had a very lucky escape as a tree trunk prevented the truck from overturning. We couldn't get it out, so five of us spent the night by the roadside while the others walked on to the camp. They sent food out at one o'clock in the morning.

At the beginning of August Harry was transferred to Tanbaya in Burma, where a hospital camp had been set up for two thousand patients. There were echoes of their horrendous march up country. Harry only had ten minutes' notice that they were leaving, so his next long diary entry was made after a friend retrieved his diary from its hiding place and brought it to him.

1 SEPTEMBER 1943

We left number 2 camp on Friday, 30th July in pouring rain and marched to number 5 camp where we stopped overnight. We left there at 3.30 AM and marched in pitch blackness for 10km. Many men fell into rivers, ditches, etc, and some men lost their kit. I was unable to see clearly in the dark, and had to hold on to the man in front like a blind man. We trucked to Kandoo, and then by train to Ronshi. We marched from there as a bridge had been swept away by the storm, and we arrived at Tanbaya where the hospital is stationed.

Conditions were slightly better here. To begin with the Japanese guards 'were a nasty bunch who led us a hell of a life', but later they got a new Japanese administration

consisting mostly of kindly-looking elderly Japs who are in stark contrast to their predecessors. They left us strictly alone, increased our food, and generally allowed us everything we asked for. The new officer, although he looks stern, is very fair, and listens attentively to all Hutch's requests, and doesn't give a propaganda speech or ask about whyfor etc.

Many of the medical staff there had malaria, and it was sometimes hard to find sufficient people to carry out essential tasks. Patients were brought in, usually in the middle of the night, so fires for the bathhouse and illuminating flares needed to be lit. They had to lift the helpless patients off the trucks and carry them into the camp hospital:

> The condition of the patients was terrible after a nightmare journey for three days in open trucks and trains, often in pouring rain. Several died on the journey, and some were brought here dead. This morning, out of a party of 114 that left no. 2 camp, 14 died on the way here and were buried en route, and 6 were brought in dead. It seems to me to be a criminal act to send these dying men on a long journey for no purpose at all, and sending no fit men or medical orderlies with them. It is absolutely amazing.

Train car, Burma Railway (1945), resembling the 'metal trucks'
in which the POWs were forcibly transported

Parties of prisoners continued to arrive – with unrealistic expectations:

14 SEPTEMBER 1943

Today a party of 200 arrived here with numerous officers, and they looked very travel-stained and hungry. They were told that they were going to open a new convalescent home!

27 SEPTEMBER 1943

Several more large parties of fit men and officers have arrived here in search of a mythical convalescent home.

More deaths were reported:

27 OCTOBER 1943

The death toll is over the 600 mark out of the original 1,600, most of the deaths now being due to chronic dysentery and malnutrition. The men who are arriving here daily are barely alive and every bone showing, Even the Japs are amazed when they see these living skeletons.

When Harry first arrived the food was quite adequate, but although the number of patients went up, the rations did not go up accordingly. After a week the total number had increased from the first group of sixty patients to 1,600, and the accommodation was extremely crowded. It was obvious that the food would have to improve to save lives. Gradually conditions got better. Stores of mosquito nets, blankets and cooking utensils were sent in along with much-needed items of clothing. There were increased supplies of food, but it did not stop the rising death tally in the hospital – more than two hundred after just eighteen days.

Harry found it difficult to sleep as his nights were very much disturbed:

1 OCTOBER 1943

Ants in their millions climb up the posts at the back of the bed, and scatter in search of food. Ants in the hair are enough to make anyone go mad. I have killed thousands, but it makes no appreciable difference to the numbers.

He was upset to hear news of the death of the last man from the concert party that had left Changi with F Force. The atrocious working conditions on the railway meant that at best there were just a few attempts to have sing-alongs around campfires. Every single account of Japanese POWs pays tribute to the entertainers who kept up morale in the most unbelievably difficult circumstances.

By the end of November the death toll in the hospital in Tanbaya had reached 640. The railway had now been completed, and most of the doctors and surviving patients were to leave for Singapore. A small contingent of medical and administrative staff were left behind in Burma to look after men who were too sick to move, but the rest were sent on the railway, built by the prisoners at such cost, to Kanburi. Three men died on the train, and there were many still suffering with malaria and dysentery:

13 NOVEMBER 1943

It is amazing that a heartbreaking march of three weeks on the way up should be accomplished in a few days on the way back.

In *Back to the Front*, Harry commented, 'I don't think really that the Japanese used the railway very much. All those lives being expended for such a thing the Japanese didn't actually make full use of. But as far as we were concerned, we were so pleased that it was built to come back on it.'

Harry was assigned to the hospital in Kanburi to care for the sick men in F Force until they were fit enough to cope with the onward journey:

28 NOVEMBER 1943

I left Tanbaya about one week ago, and after a very uncomfortable journey by train which lasted four and a half days, we arrived at Kanburi. We were crowded 33 to a truck and I sat on my pack as there was no room for my feet on the floor. The sores on my buttocks became inflamed and made sitting an absolute torture. We were greeted at the station by a large bevy of female vendors of eggs, bananas, coffee etc, and we indulged in an orgy of spending. Up until then we had very little opportunity of spending our Thai money. We marched to the fit camp where we met the officers and ORs who had been left behind. Yesterday I was transferred to this hospital a few km away where H Force had collected and which is to be the home of F Force sick until they are well enough to be sent to Singapore. We left behind in Burma about 250 men who are unfit to travel. Probably time alone will solve the problem of their ultimate fate.

Finally, they travelled back to Singapore. They were taken from the station to Changi by truck in the early hours of 21 December 1943, Harry's thirty-third birthday. The clock chimed midnight as they passed through the silent, dark streets, and Harry told his fellow officers the significance of the date. Immediately they started singing 'Happy Birthday', and the Japanese driver stopped the truck to see what was going on. He could not understand why they seemed so happy, and Harry said the driver clearly thought the British were quite mad!

In Harry's dictated section of his diaries he added the following comments:

F Force comprised 3,600 Australians and 3,400 British who went up country to work on the Burma–Thai Railway. Our furthest camp was in Burma at Tanbaya which is north of the Three Pagodas Pass at the Burma–Thai border. 3,900 men returned, a death rate of 45%. F Force suffered such large casualties mainly because of the cholera epidemic combined with the harsh conditions and a diet which had a severe deficiency of vitamin B.

Looking back, it seems inconceivable that we believed the Japs when they told us the move would be to convalescent and rest homes – to the extent that a third of the Force were unfit men looking forward to a chance to recover their health! We happily transported lighting sets, pianos and other musical instruments in the expectation of continuing our concert parties in our new camp. These were soon dumped along the way during the dreadful march north.

The epithets 'ill-starred' and 'ill-fated' are often ascribed to F Force. Unlike the parties that had been sent up country earlier, F Force was not deemed to be a working party. A high percentage of the POWs allocated to this force were, for a number of reasons, regarded as not fit enough to be transferred to working areas. They were encouraged to go, persuaded by the false promises of a better climate to enable the sick to recuperate. It is quite astonishing that there were any survivors at all.

13

The Event We Have Been Looking Forward to So Eagerly

Once the prisoners were back in Changi, life became comparatively more normal. Their old quarters were being converted into an aerodrome, so the POWs were housed temporarily in huts and houses before being moved into the civilian Changi Gaol. The civilians, who had previously been housed there were relocated to the Sime Road Camp. A thousand British prisoners were crammed inside the jail:

13 MAY 1944

I never imagined that I would one day come to live in a jail. Two days ago I was ordered to move with a party of 1000 British to Changi Gaol. I was very sorry to leave my last Mess as food and accommodation were very good. We marched here and settled down inside the jail, the men going to small cells and the officers going to large hospital cells holding 14–20. Initially there is a depressing atmosphere about the place which takes some time to get used to. Two high walls surrounding the jail guarded by Nips, all windows are shut in with bars and wire mesh. All windows are enclosed with bars and wires and one gets a feeling of being hemmed in. I feel it particularly after the open air comfort of the last billet. My first morning sick parade was an absolute shambles. 700 sick fighting their way in simultaneously.

Three weeks later, Harry was reaccommodated into one of the huts just outside the jail. It was also very cramped, the officers 'lying cheek by jowl and some are double berthing in order to give themselves more floor space'. There was a spate of remarkable orders with pernickety details about the dressing of beds and instructions that all clothes lines had to run north–south. Harry had no idea if these were at the instigation of the Japanese or the British.

A month after this he was moved once more into one of three houses known as Harley Street, as they were used for sick officers and the MOs. Here they had more space and gardens where they could grow vegetables, including tapioca root and tomatoes. Once a week the crops needed fertilising:

22 DECEMBER 1944

This morning in the half-light before dawn while it

was raining and cold, I had to get up and collect buckets of urine and take them along to the garden. This afternoon I am on a trailer party to collect lalang [a type of weed] for compost.

Although the rations continued to be very poor, and there were still incidents of torture and deprivation, conditions were never as bad as those up country. However, the Japanese never let them forget they were still prisoners and had frequent roll calls where the men were left standing for hours on end:

> On two occasions recently we had midnight roll calls extending over a couple of hours due to suspected escapes. No-one had escaped and on the second occasion the missing man was found dead in a bore hole.

The POWs settled into a routine, renewing the Changi University and the wonderful shows that kept up the men's morale. Harry praised an excellent production of *Hay Fever* which had a professional actor as the main lead. Unfortunately they had to close one of the theatres:

19 MARCH 1945

The Playhouse Theatre was first ordered to be pulled down and then altered to close down because certain items in the present show appear to have offended the Nips (it is only an excuse again). This is a great pity for the good theatre is our main source of entertainment.

He attended two lectures given by an Italian officer on modern submarine warfare:

24 JULY 1945

It is a strange state of affairs when we hear one of our former enemies talk about his part in the undersea warfare against our shipping and an amazing thing to hear the cheers at the end for a man who recently was helping to sink our merchant fleet.

This reference to an Italian officer in Changi may seem quite puzzling, but there were two Italian submarines in Singapore when Italy capitulated in September 1943. They were given the choice of pro- or anti-Mussolini allegiance, and about a third chose the latter in spite of the probable consequence of imprisonment.

Harry still read in his leisure time and played a nightly game of bridge. He took pleasure in a good debate and went to one titled 'If we want peace, we must prepare for war'. The motion was carried.

Harry had built up a collection of artwork given to him by fellow POWs. Typical of the British sense of humour is a drawing by T. A. J. Wickham titled 'The Decline and Fall of a Tin Hat'. It chronicles the imaginary stages of alternative uses of the soldier's tin hat, finishing as a receptacle for stools held by a skeletal prisoner outside a laboratory.

The prisoners were allowed to go down to the sea, which was very beneficial. They not only welcomed the opportunity to go swimming but could also bring back wood for the fires and coconuts for the mess.

While F Force was up country, there had been a daring escape by ten men who hoped to tell the world about the brutal conditions on the railway. Only four survived, including Harry's friend Jim Bradley:

5 JANUARY 1944

They are very lucky to be alive after their most amazing adventures. They had to hack their way through thick jungle and climb high ranges of mountains daily. This slowed their speed and they ran short of food, and for the last three weeks of their journey they starved. Four officers died, one by one, and were left – a tragic end – somewhere in the jungle. They built a raft when they came to a river but the current was strong and carried them over rocks and falls and finally it smashed in midstream. They were flung into the water and had to swim for their lives. They later saw some native hunters up a canal who looked after them for a few days but finally gave them up to the Japs.

The survivors were brought back for interrogation and trial.

It was expected that they would be tortured or executed or both, but miraculously they were sentenced to eight or nine years' penal servitude in Outram Road Gaol. This was infamous as a place of starvation and terror, but they were all released on grounds of ill health after a couple of months and were sent back to hospital in Changi.

Harry was very happy that he could visit Jim Bradley and the other escapees in hospital. In fact, Jim Bradley credited his survival to Harry, who, before the escape, had given him some sulphonamides to treat two small tropical ulcers. He put these on each ulcer, binding them with mosquito netting, and thus averted a potential life-threatening deterioration.

'The Decline and Fall of a Tin Hat.'
Cartoon by T. A. J. Wickham, 1945

An unpleasant incident happened to Padre Cordingly during this period. He had to spend two days in a pit handcuffed to an acting sergeant for carrying letters from one camp to another containing alleged news. This was not the first such episode for the Padre. While they were on the railway in Thailand he had offered a similar service. Since most men had no clothes but a tattered loincloth, and he owned a pair of shorts, he had been given notes scribbled by men asking for news of friends. Unfortunately, the Padre and an Indian doctor with the party were stopped and searched, and accused of being spies. They were handcuffed to each other and thrown into a pit. While it was still dark a young Japanese guard lowered a ladder into the pit and offered them sweet tea and two bananas. The Padre was released the next day. There is no doubt the young soldier would have been executed if his humanitarian action had been discovered.

Harry was kept busy with his medical duties, caring for patients on different wards. He found the work on the tuberculosis ward particularly interesting, extending his knowledge of this disease. Malaria was rife, with a shortage of quinine, and there were still many cases of dysentery and stomatitis. Their diet continued to be very short of vitamin B, especially because they now had no rice polishings, resulting in a greater incidence of diseases caused by vitamin deficiency such as beriberi. Harry himself had spells of poor health, including a bad bout of malaria and an acute attack of bacterial dysentery, both leaving him feeling very ill for several days.

In May 1944, the remainder of the survivors who had stayed up country returned to Changi:

3 MAY 1944

The death roll for F and H Forces must now be nearly 5,000. Out of the 1,600 who went to No. 2 camp, there are only 185 alive. This figure should make someone in Tokyo sit up.

Very gradually conditions improved. The Japanese allowed them more Red Cross parcels, sharing one parcel between seven men. Harry said the American parcels had a good variety of tins containing health foods and vitamins. The prisoners also received batches of old mail which had accumulated in their absence up country – Harry was given eleven letters, all about a year old.

In August 1944 the Japanese provided materials to build a small synagogue, which was named Ohel Jacob:

30 AUGUST 1944

Last Saturday night I was a spectator of a rather unique ceremony – the dedication of the recently built shul in the gaol called Ohel Jacob. Everything was built and prepared by the boys themselves. A representation of the tablets above the ark was painted realistically and a decorated (suitably) curtain hung in front of an imaginary ark.

This fulfilled the need for a permanent place of worship for the Jewish POWs. It became a haven of peace in what was at the time a very overcrowded prison. The synagogue was also useful as a venue for Changi University:

> The synagogue is used for lectures etc during the week and it is rather amusing to see the location of a maths lecture given on the board as Ohel Jacob.

Harry himself gave a couple of lectures on medical topics in the synagogue, including one on humour in medicine.

Harry attended his first Jewish funeral as a POW:

9 MARCH 1945

I went to Jack Baker's funeral yesterday. He was a boy I got to know up-country and he did me many good turns. He was very ill up-country, bacterial diarrhoea etc and developed TB after arriving back here in Changi. When he died all the Volunteer officers and many of the men of his unit in addition to all his Jewish friends turned up for the funeral. [Camp commandant] Takahashi and [Lt-Col Thomas] Newey [the Japanese-appointed commander of the POWs] stood outside the Gaol and saluted the cortege – the Nip guards presented arms and the long procession moved slowly out of the Gaol to begin its two mile walk to the cemetery. It must have been strange for the gentiles listening to a Jewish funeral with its traditional wailing melodies. His father was informed the day after his son died. What a family tragedy – imprisonment and death.

Harry celebrated his thirty-fourth birthday on 21 December 1944 with his friends:

> Well! Another birthday spent on foreign soil has come and gone. I gave a little party for 10 people in the billet – Wilkie, Titus, Simmie, Padre, Dixie, Bill English, Hecht, Burgess, Delamos and me. Owing to the scarcity of foodstuffs I had a pie made of tapioca root, tomatoes (own grown) and 2 tins of veg soup and numerous extras. Ted – our Messing officer – made it himself and made a jolly good job of it. It was very tasty and we all felt happily replete at the end. I provided coffee and gula and cheroots. We all had a very good evening under the circumstances. I keep hoping that each birthday here will be the last one but I have now ceased to speculate about the future.

The Japanese cancelled a grand fairground planned by the officers to celebrate Christmas, but the POWs did eat well:

1 JANUARY 1945

Xmas passed as usual with the traditional stuffing of oneself. There was an enormous meal on Xmas night after a big tiffin and tea and consequently most of it was left. Some including the Xmas cake was eaten the following day. I think that in a POW camp where rations are poor, the extra food should be spread over a few days and ease the shock of going back to ordinary meals.

More than three hundred toys were made by the POWs and sent over to Sime Road Camp for the children of the civilian prisoners at Christmas.

On 1 January 1945 Harry wrote:

Nearly three years have passed since I started this diary and the worst pessimist here won't predict another full year.

Finally, in August 1945 the long-circulating rumours that the war in the Far East was ending were confirmed. This is Harry's last diary entry:

25 AUGUST 1945

The event we have been looking forward to so eagerly for the past 3½ years has now taken place and with a suddenness that surprised us all. Early morning of August 11th found most of the camp up, in little groups discussing the rumour that the Emperor had agreed to accept the terms of the Potsdam conference. When this was confirmed later in the day we began to make plans for celebrations and an early evacuation.

Most of the tapioca root in the gardens was pulled up and consumed over 3 days and our little conclave Dixie, Doug Walker, John McNeath and I had 3 successive evening parties when we opened our reserve tins of food (fish and meat), condensed milk and emergency chocolate. We also pulled up all our greens, roots etc and had continuous food orgies. But day succeeded day and we still had Japanese roll call parades and had to salute the Nips and generally carried on as previously. This was a bit of an anti-climax and we had a bit of a shock when the local commander said that he intended to fight on and defend the island. However an order from the Emperor to cease fire ultimately reached the island after 10 days of ups and downs of spirits.

By a gradual process the local Nips became convinced that the war was over and then restrictions etc were slowly relaxed. But during the past 3 days since Dillon has nominally taken over the camp, food and clothing has poured in. We each have been supplied with a complete outfit of clothing – cheap Nip stuff – the rations have been pushed up to 3000 calories and fish and meat. Red Cross parcels are piling into the Gaol. 1/20th a parcel per man per day is being issued and cigarettes etc at frequent intervals. Nussbaum put on a party in the shool [synagogue] and a thanksgiving service is being held shortly.

We now have official printed news bulletins after years of whispered extracts and are awaiting Lord

Louis' [Mountbatten's] arrival eagerly. The outlying working camps have concentrated round the Gaol area and we are packed like sardines. The hospital has over 2000 patients and there is a severe outbreak of gastroenteritis to complicate matters. We are pushing vitamin B etc into patients but there are several cases of sudden death due to heart failure which are baffling the experts.

We follow all references to POWs in the news very carefully and there is much speculation as to our future as each successive speaker seems to have different ideas on the subject. It seems however that we will be taken back home as soon as possible by air or by sea as transport becomes available.

During this exciting waiting period we rush to the doorways every time we hear a plane in the sky hoping to see for the first time for over 3 years the tricolour that means liberation and freedom for us.

39, Hyde Park Gate,
London, S.W.7.

27th October 1945.

Dear Silman,

    I am writing to welcome you home
and to say how very glad we are to see
you safely back. I know you have had a
trying time and I want to thank you for
the great work so many of you did under
the most difficult circumstances and with
little or no equipment to succour your
fellow captives.

    It has been very highly appreciated
by the public at home and by the Army.
We, your brother officers, feel you have
nobly maintained the highest traditions
of our profession and our Corps and we
are very proud of you.

    May you soon be restored to your
usual vigour.

        Yours sincerely,

Captain H.Silman, R.A.M.C.,
22, Grange Avenue,
LEEDS, 7.

War Office 'welcome home' letter, 1945

Epilogue

While Harry was waiting to be repatriated he wrote this letter home:

Sept 6/45

My dear Mam, Dad and all the family,

How can I begin to express in this, my first letter home after 3½ years durance fairly vile, what has transpired during that time. So much has shaken the Silman frame that when we are gathered round the fireside in the old homestead and pass round the brandy, I will recount to you such tales that will make you rock on your heels, and you will begin to wonder whether or not you had given birth to a second Dumas or Munchausen.

I expect that so much will be written by so many by the time I get home, that it will only need my corroboration and a few personal details to set the seal. However let me start with a few facts about me. I am exuding rude health and rice from every pore, and during the past four weeks have put on over 20lbs in weight. I spend most of my waking hours taking out the tucks in my pants. I am now back to my old weight and have regained my manly figure and vigour. One naturally loses weight on a restricted Asiatic diet such as we have been pushing back for the past four years, but there is now a superabundance of good food pouring in on us.

We have now had the ball and chain hacked off, and ships and planes are daily unloading supplies and troops of all descriptions. We are slowly getting used to a non-POW life, and still feel embarrassed when a Nip salutes us. We are hoping to leave here in a few days and proceed direct to the UK, but things are very confused at the present and we do not know exactly what is to happen to us.

As you probably know, in spite of the strict censorship prevailing at the time, I was nabbed by the Nips in Feb 42, and have been resting here all the time except for a short trip up country to Thailand and Burma lasting 9 months, during which time we constructed a model railway.

This interim period of waiting before we are bunged home is being made very pleasant by all sorts of organisations doing their best to provide us with food, clothing, toilet requisites etc. and we look like being re-equipped from head to foot before we are through with these blokes.

I hope that all at home are in the pink, and although I have been away from no. 22 for nearly 4 years, expect to find it unchanged except for the books not being tidied and replaced in the bookcase, and Mam's teeth possibly in a different glass due to the other one being worn out. I imagine with the concentration of forces at no. 22, conditions may be a little crowded, but I wouldn't notice that now – interval for a spot of bitter laughter. I anticipate getting a few months' leave (with pay) after my return to England, before I recommence the daily toil. You might cut out the odd advert from the Wanted column – if anyone wants a doctor who has been sober and out of mischief for the past few years. I have done all sorts of jobs so am not very particular now.

Writing this letter has its difficulties as I am shooing away mosquitoes with one hand, stopping would-be purloiners of my ink bottle with the other and trying to concentrate in spite of 2 loudspeakers blaring out the news and events of the day. One of the things we appreciate most is listening to the BBC again, and getting a regular up-to-date news service. The Nips neglected to lay this on for us.

I will write again as soon as poss.

Love from Harry

Harry met his beloved wife Dorothea within a few weeks of his return to Leeds. She said that although he was jaundiced and skinny, she fell immediately in love with him because he made her laugh. They were very happily married for nearly sixty years. His three children – Jackie, Marilyn and Alan – gave him the warm family life he had doubted would ever happen, and his contentment was later completed by cherished grandchildren and great-grandchildren. He cared about each member of his family, including, as he put it, everyone mad enough to have married into it. He derived tremendous pleasure from our achievements. Our happiness was his happiness, our sorrows equally his sorrows.

He worked as a GP until he was in his mid-seventies, and it is clear from the testimonials and letters he received on his retirement that he was a much-loved doctor.

Harry always played down the harrowing events of his wartime years with a dry sense of humour, as can be seen in his first letter home. I remember we were occasionally told we should finish what was on our plates as 'your father would have been very happy to have had a meal like this during the war', but otherwise our memories are of a happy person with a positive outlook on life.

When he died aged ninety-four, Harry was still the kind, caring human being who was an integral part of all our lives. He was genuinely interested in people. Even on a casual level, while many of us listen to others with half an ear, my father would ask pertinent questions and give considered advice. He was an engaging conversationalist, and it was a pleasure to be in his company. Harry had an open mind, embracing new ideas and technology with enthusiasm. He was totally fascinated by the power of the internet and quickly understood that Google could find details on all medical problems, however obscure.

Harry had the ability to see the funny side of life. I know his positive outlook and sense of humour helped him (and many others) to survive the war years. All the family would go to him for wise counsel, and, until the final few months of his life, he was always smiling, quick with a pun or corny joke.

And, remarkably, he still enjoyed rice ...

Harry at the turn of the twenty-first century,
aged eighty-nine

ABBREVIATIONS AND GLOSSARY

AA/ack-ack	anti-aircraft gunfire
ACG	Assistant Chaplain General
ADC	Army Dental Corps
ADMS	Assistant Director Medical Services
ARP	air raid precaution
atap	roofing material made from palm tree leaves
barracks	large building(s) to house soldiers
batman	officer's personal assistant
billet	soldiers' living quarters
BEF	British Expeditionary Force
Boches	Germans (from French slang; derogatory)
C-in-C	commander-in-chief
CO	commanding officer
DADMS	Deputy Assistant Director Medical Services
dixies	huge cooking pots for mass catering
Div/divn	division
FA	field ambulance
GOC	General Officer Commanding
HQ	headquarters
Hun	mild derogatory slang for Germans
IJA	Imperial Japanese Army

India Lines	barracks and training grounds used by Indian regiments of the British Indian Army
Jerries	slang for Germans
K	khaki
KD	khaki drill (military uniform)
latrines	army toilets. The quickest to construct were a deep pit or trench and partly covering it with wooden planks. They were not as hygienic as the Indian-style latrines – the squat toilets seen widely in Asia today.
Mess	military dining-room
MI	medical inspection (MI room was equivalent to a surgery)
MO	medical officer (i.e. doctor)
NCO	non-commissioned officer. NCOs usually reach reach officer level by working through promotions, unlike others who come into the army at officer level.
Nips	pejorative term for Japanese people (from *Nippon*, Japanese for 'Japan')
OC	Officer Commanding
OR	other ranks (i.e. the ordinary soldiers who ranked below officers and NCOs)

Padre	army chaplain
Padang	playing field
PMC	President of the Mess Committee
POW	prisoner of war
RAF	Royal Air Force
RAMC	Royal Army Medical Corps
RAOC	Royal Army Ordnance Corps
RAP	regimental aid post (i.e. first-aid station)
RASC	Royal Army Service Corps
RE	Royal Engineers
RNF	Royal Northumberland Fusiliers
RP	rice polishings
S	Singapore
Sappers	soldiers in the Corps of Royal Engineers
Tommies	slang for British soldiers, originating in the nineteenth century with 'Thomas Atkins', a name supplied by the Army as an example when filling in official forms
topee	lightweight helmet-shaped hat offering protection
warrant officer	highest level of NCO

SOURCES AND NOTES

Books

Adams, Geoffrey Pharaoh, *No Time for Geishas*, London: Leo Cooper, 1973. A Japanese POW. Jim Bradley regarded him as one of the greatest authorities on the Thailand-Burma Railway

Barclay, Brigadier C. N., *The History of the Royal Northumberland Fusiliers in the Second World War*, London: William Clowes, 1952. This was the basis of much of Paul Reynolds' comprehensive research into the RNF's time in France in the days leading up to the retreat from Dunkirk – a personal account with a focus on his father-in-law, Padre Eric Cordingly, who was attached (like Harry) to the RNF for the whole of the war. The editor thanks Paul Reynolds for permission to use his research, which informed the historical content of Chapter 1.

Bradley, James, *Towards the Setting Sun: An Escape from the Thailand–Burma Railway, 1943*, Chichester: Phillimore & Co., 1982. All references to James Bradley's words are taken from this publication.

Cordingly, Eric, *Down to Bedrock: The Diary and Secret Notes of a Far East Prisoner of War Chaplain 1942–45*, Louise Cordingly, ed., Norwich: Art Angels, 2013. All extracts from Padre Cordingly's diaries are taken from this publication.

Cordingly, Louise, ed., *Echoes of Captivity*, London: High Winds Publishing, 2020. This book, edited by Louise Cordingly, daughter of Harry's fellow POW and friend Padre Eric Cordingly, contains thirty-four interviews with children of Far East World War Two POWs.

"Fusilier George" in France, 1940. Being A Story of the 9th Battalion, Royal Northumberland Fusiliers, April and May 1940, Dover: G. W. Grigg and Son, 1941. 'Fusilier George' probably represents two or three officers who wrote this accurate, occasionally colourful account based on the RNF's own *War Diaries*, and had it printed privately.

Radio

The Reunion: Far East Prisoners of War, presented by Sue MacGregor, BBC Radio 4, Whistledown, first broadcast 26 April 2015.

Television

Back to the Front: Doctors at War, Yorkshire Television, 2003, XYTV Productions, director: Diane Myers. The documentary chronicles the experiences of six medical officers during World War Two.

CREDITS

p. 106   Courtesy of the Imperial War Museum (Art. IWM ART 1541729)

p. 126   The Private Papers of Captain H. Silman, Imperial War Museum, London

pp. 128–9 Maps by www.friedbanana.co.uk

p. 141   Courtesy of the author

p. 145   Unknown author, *"Trein op de houten spoorbrug bij km. 155 tussen Tampi en Hintoku in de Birma-Siamspoorweg in Siam"*, KITLV 25518 (between 1942–3), Creative Commons CC BY 4.0

p. 159   Australian War Memorial, AWM collection 157866.

p. 170   The Private Papers of Captain H. Silman, Imperial War Museum, London

p. 178   Courtesy of the author

p. 183   Courtesy of the author